WAYFARER BOOKS and *WAYFARER MAGAZINE* are based in the San Juan Mountains at the gateway to Mesa Verde, on the lands of the Ancestral Pueblo, the Southern Ute, the Mountain Ute–the *Weeminuche'*, the *Diné* (Navajo), and the San Juan Southern Paiute Nations. We honor the generations of Indigenous communities who have lived in, stewarded, and maintained these lands for thousands of years. We recognize that this land was taken through colonization and displacement, and we acknowledge the ongoing presence and contributions of Indigenous peoples, past, and present. As a company rooted in stories and knowledge, we commit to listening, learning, and supporting Indigenous voices, sovereignty, and wealth redistribution.

I0555316

we are on native land.

wayfarer

WHOLESALE INQUIRIES? *WAYFARER MAGAZINE* is published by the Wayfarer Group. You can find our books available via Ingram, offered with standard trade terms and lifetime returnability. With printing bases in the US, the EU, the UK, and Australia, Wayfarer has the capability to fulfill orders globally.

Our titles are available wherever books are sold in paperback, ebook, and audiobook. Find our books at local Indies, Bookshop.org, iTunes, Barnes & Noble, Amazon > US & International, or direct at wayfarerbookstore.com

FOUNDER AND EDITOR-IN-CHIEF

CONNOR WOLFE (THEY/THEM)

EDITORS

THEODORE RICHARDS (HE/HIM)

GWENDOLYN MORGAN (SHE/HER)

HEIDI BARR (SHE/HER)

IRIS GRAVILLE (SHE/HER)

THOMAS LLYOD QUALLS (HE/HIM)

ROBERT BRODER (HE/HIM)

WILL FALK (HE/HIM)

FRANCSCA G. VARELA (SHE/HER)

PUBLISHING HOUSE & MAGAZINE

ORDERS@WAYFARERBOOK.ORG

PR@WAYFARERBOOKS.ORG

MANAGINGEDITOR@WAYFARERBOOKS.ORG

FOLLOW US

INSTAGRAM > @THEWAYFARER_MAG

INSTAGRAM > @ WAYFARER.BOOKS

BLUESKY > @WAYFARERBOOKS.BSKY.SOCIAL

SUBSTACK > WAYFARERMAGAZINE.COM

"*Wayfarer* will not simply publish books. We will ignite cultural fire where we can.
We will stand as a home for the wild, the silenced, the feral, and the broken-hearted truth-tellers.
We will put literature back in the streets, in the mouths of the people, in the wild spaces where
real language lives. We will be a movement, not just a press."

—Connor Wolfe, Founder & Publisher, *Wayfarer*

FROM THE EDITOR

Dear Wayfarers,

This year asked us who we are when the unthinkable happens...again.

Wayfarer was founded to chart the road to change and to map the routes between us so we can better understand ourselves and the world we share. Over the last twelve months, that mission sharpened into an obligation.

As a trans-owned publishing house during a rise in fascism, we are more than a magazine now; we are a public record that says *we were here, we are here, and we will be here tomorrow*. In this global moment, a trans press cannot merely publish what is marketable or strictly brand-aligning; we must extend a hand to those whose existence is threatened and who have something to say to us from the margins.

Our focus as a magazine now is a stand against erasure. When the machine of fascism tries to censor the human story to a single column, our pages must widen. When laws are drafted to silence us, we must answer with a rallying cry of voices.

This issue gathers a year of protest and persistence, but it does not only look back. It looks toward the future our communities are already building. The pieces in this issue are not identical in tone—some rage, some pray, some laugh, but all are worthy of being heard.

In these pages, you will meet people who risked being known in an effort to lay down language as a bridge. Such actions are not small; each poem and essay are coordinates that lead toward understanding lives different from your own.

If you have been in the streets, we see you. If you have been at home, tending to your own becoming, we see you. If you are bone-deep tired, we see you, too. Movements require surge and rest. The fight against fascism is not a season; it's a practice.

In solidarity

—CONNOR WOLFE

CONTENTS

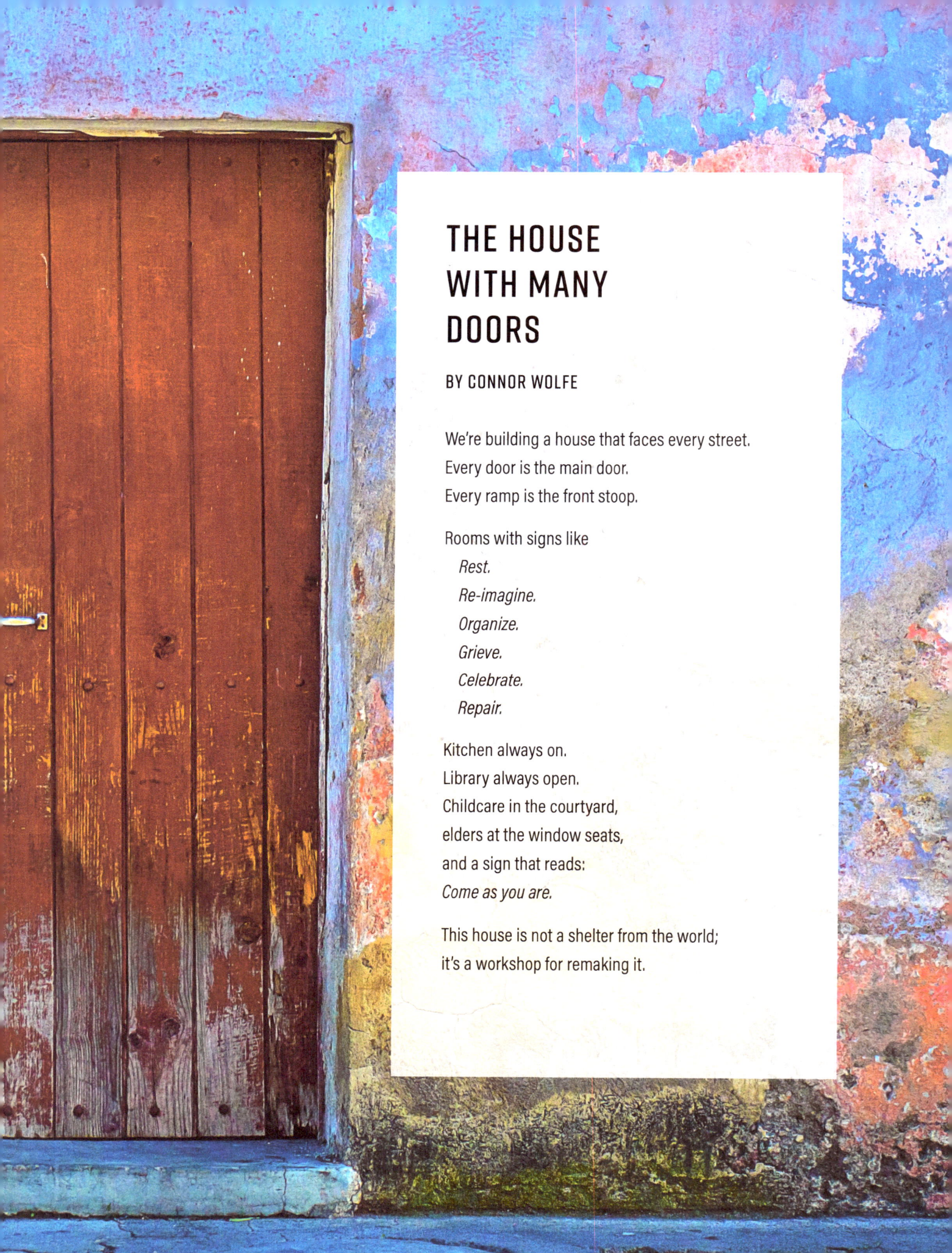

THE HOUSE WITH MANY DOORS

BY CONNOR WOLFE

We're building a house that faces every street.
Every door is the main door.
Every ramp is the front stoop.

Rooms with signs like
    Rest.
    Re-imagine.
    Organize.
    Grieve.
    Celebrate.
    Repair.

Kitchen always on.
Library always open.
Childcare in the courtyard,
elders at the window seats,
and a sign that reads:
Come as you are.

This house is not a shelter from the world;
it's a workshop for remaking it.

You've Done This Before

AN ESSAY BY SENIOR EDITOR, THEODORE RICHARDS

An excerpt from *What Happened to Icarus: Encountering the Unfathomable in a World in Crisis*

(WAYFARER BOOKS, MARCH 2026)

"You're gonna have to catch the baby!"

My wife's voice was loud and strained, with a hint of panic. I continued to fumble with the showerhead. Moments before, when she'd realized she was in labor, she'd asked me to attach the hose to the showerhead in order to fill the birthing tub while we waited for the midwife. Our third daughter, Vismaya, whom we'd never expected, was a planned homebirth; but the plan was to have a midwife present.

I fumbled some more. There are things I am good at, things that don't particularly faze me. Plumbing and anything that has to do with taking things apart and putting them back together are not on that list. I let out a sigh of relief. I much preferred to catch a baby than reconfigure the plumbing.

Ari's voice was letting out sounds that had grown increasingly, desperately, primal as Cosima, now seven, came into the bathroom. We'd welcomed her participation in the birth, but she looked a little scared. It was the sounds her mother was making. "You don't have to stay," I said. She went back to her room, got under the covers, and waited for her sister to arrive.

I washed my hands. It seemed like the thing to do. Seemed medical.

"I don't think I can do this!" my wife exclaimed, voice cracking just a bit. She must have been thinking some unarticulated version of this: The midwife isn't here and I am left in the hands of a man who can't unscrew a showerhead, who can't even turn on the television without me. This is why women used to die in childbirth in the 1800s. And I did always joke that, without my wife, our home is like the 1800s, so limited are my technical capabilities.

But there was nothing technical, or even medical, about this birth. I looked her in the eye. "You can do this," I said. "You've done this before." Like this was what we'd been waiting to do since that day, so many years ago, on the porch: to give birth. Like this was the rhyme she'd been waiting to spit but couldn't quite find the words until now.

She focused on pushing. I felt beneath where she squatted. Drops of blood fell over my hands, then more. Then the head. The head is the hardest part, the most painful part, as anyone knows who has given birth or witnessed a birth. It is the uniquely human part of the process; our big heads contain the minds that contain universes, from the cave paintings to Coltrane. We think we are different merely because our big heads make us smarter. But the human baby is born earlier, less developed, than it should be. Any longer a gestation period and the head would never get through. So we don't get up running like zebras.

Those who have witnessed birth know this, too: The human baby is utterly dependent. Because of the abbreviated gestation, required by our big heads, we are biologically required to love our babies. We are only human because we can create community and care for one another. Our big heads can write symphonies; but they can also create nuclear bombs. Care is just as important as innovation.

The head came out, and along with it a deluge of liquids. I held the little body as it slid out into my arms, bloody and gasping for air. Like her parents. Like the whole world into which she'd come.

You've done this before.

My wife sat on the toilet and put the child to her breast. We cried at the bloody and awesome beauty. She was our beautiful, cosmic surprise. I had caught her, our unexpected third daughter.

This is how the universe works: We didn't know that we'd have three daughters, but the world is unimaginable without each of them. There is a perfection in this, a thing to listen to in the world. Their days are spent in a maelstrom of creative energy, creating, imagining, making worlds. Three girls. This is something in itself to listen to.

When I close my eyes, I see those drops of blood on my hands, like the raindrops falling into my hands on the Mozambican beach. To live in this world is to have blood on your hands; to be alive is to have the courage not to turn away, because something is being birthed out of the bloody mess.

I caught her. Perhaps, one day, when I fall and fail in countless ways, she will catch me, too. For we spend so much of our lives trying to fly, trying to touch the sun. Trying to be like a god. But the real story always begins with a fall; the real story only begins with descent.

Theodore Richards (he/him) is an educator, poet, and philosopher, and the founder of The Chicago Wisdom Project. His work is dedicated to re-imagining education and creating new narratives about our place in the world. He has received degrees from various institutions, including the University of Chicago and The California Institute of Integral Studies, but has learned just as much studying the martial art of Bagua; teaching in various settings and students; and as a traveler from the Far East to the Middle East, from southern Africa to the South Pacific. He is the author of eight books and numerous literary awards, including two Nautilus Book Awards and three Independent Publisher Awards. He lives on the south side of Chicago with his wife and three daughters.

INTRODUCING

uncharted.

Behind every artist, writer, and dreamer lies a terrain of choices, risks, and discoveries that can't be plotted in advance. To create is to wander into the unknown, guided less by certainty than by curiosity. Each guest is asked the same ten questions, but their answers reveal something far greater—an unfiltered glimpse into the raw, unpredictable, and deeply personal terrain of a creative life.

Created by **Connor Wolfe (they/them)**, founder of Wayfarer Books and *Wayfarer Magazine*, "Uncharted" is an invitation to step off the map and explore what it means to live, work, and create beyond the expected.

uncharted

with Pádraig Ó Tuama

ON PRESENCE, REBELLION, AND THE MAPS OF CREATIVITY

Today we're joined by poet and theologian Pádraig Ó Tuama (he/him), whose work explores the intersections of language, power, conflict, and religion. He's not only a gifted writer on the page, but also a compelling speaker, teacher, and facilitator of groups. Many will know him as the host of Poetry Unbound from *On Being* Studios.

From 2014 ᴛᴏ 2019, Pádraig led the Corrymeela Community—Ireland's oldest peace and reconciliation organization. His academic background is equally rich: he holds undergraduate and postgraduate degrees in theology, professional qualifications in conflict mediation, and a PhD in Poetry and Theology from the University of Glasgow. Looking ahead, he'll be serving as a visiting scholar at Columbia University's Centre for Cooperation and Conflict Resolution through the autumn terms of 2024 to 2028.

To give you a sense of his impact, BBC journalist William Crawley once introduced him at a TEDx talk by saying, "He's probably the best public speaker I know." And as *The New Yorker's* Eliza Griswold observed, for Pádraig, "Poetry is the language the heart speaks not when t reaches for some externalized divinity but when it seeks to understand itself."

1. WHAT'S LIGHTING YOU UP CREATIVELY RIGHT NOW?

At this very moment, I am looking out at a tree, and in the tree is a bird. I'm traveling, so I'm around birdlife I don't recognize. The bird has a yellow beak, and is sitting on a cluster of berries protruding from a tall slender palm tree. The berries are red and the bird's plucking them off one by one, eating some, spitting others out, shitting merrily as it goes. Now it's hopped to a twig so light, I can barely believe it can sustain the weight of even a light bird. And now—just seconds later—its flown to a large horizontal palm frond extending perpendicularly from a more sturdy tree. Somewhere else another bird is singing. In fact, I can hear three: something dove-like, something like a song, and something throaty and husky. Interestingly, I can't hear the jungle fowl who—at any point of the day—can release their explosions of noise without warning. I've just counted, and in the space of five seconds, I could count ten different shapes of leaves and foliage on the immediate plants and trees and palms near me. And now, as if I've summoned them by writing about them, one of those damned fowl has crowed. I was awake early this morning, 4.15am or so, and the crowing started then, and it's now six hours later, and it's still *pandemoniuming* its way through the waking hours. The male jungle fowl has a slightly shorter crow than that of the domestic rooster—rising with objection, but without the elongated end. Right now, another bird—hidden too, and utterly new to me—is squeaking near me. It goes from a whistle to a nasal squeak, then back again. Fresh as the morning.

2. WHAT'S THE LAST THING THAT TRULY CAPTIVATED YOU—AN IDEA, A PLACE, A PIECE OF ART, A POEM, A MOMENT?

The last thing? That bird. And the garden. And the light on the mountain last night when the sun was going down. I'm on Maui, staying in the house that Paula and W.S. Merwin built and lived in for many years. It's run now by the Merwin Conservancy, a living land modeled after poetry, place, preservation. They— fools!— invite writers to stay for a few weeks while working on a project. (I've threatened to never leave). Merwin had purchased two acres about fifty years ago, with plans to build a house and plant on what was deemed wasteland. It's now a rainforest of palm trees—some of them endangered—and birdlife and insect life (the little bastards love my milky blood, it seems).

3. WHAT'S A RECENT EXPERIENCE THAT MADE YOU FEEL DEEPLY PRESENT?

It started to rain last evening and continued all night. When I got up this morning, I made tea (Assam, with milk, in a flask to keep it warm) and sat on the lanai nearest to what was Paula Merwin's office. I closed my eyes, listened to the rain, tried to recall what I'd read of the Stoics yesterday, and thought about the cardinal virtues (justice, wisdom, courage and moderation), but alongside that, I thought of the etymology of cardinal (it does not, as I'd wondered, share etymology with cardiac) and then—how could I not?—I thought of the cardinals I've seen flying around the trees during the week since I've arrived. The sound of the rain was like a permanent rhyme, a percussion, without metrical beat, but with a pulse as indigenous as that of the heart. And then I thought of how the Stoics were mostly interested in ways of being present, without allowing flights of uncontrollable things to take control. They didn't think they were the first to state their wisdom: their wisdom has found voice in all human cultures, I imagine.

My grandmother—in the midst of a long life with sorrow—loved the occasion for a song, or a cigarette, or a baby's smile. And there were plenty. Babies that is. I've just counted: I was one of eighteen cousins born in eighteen years. She was present this morning too, although she's never been to Hawai'i, and is dead many years. She was wearing the patterned housecoat she always wore, pottering about, uninterested in me, setting the butter out to soften in the warm.

PHOTOS BY DAVID PUGH

4. WHAT'S A PIECE OF ART, A BOOK, OR A CONVERSATION THAT'S BEEN LIVING IN YOUR MIND RENT-FREE?

I've been captivated by "Water" — Haleh Liza Gafori's most recent translation of Rumi's work (NYRB, 2025). I don't believe in God (believe isn't a strong enough verb for me), but I like reading some of the writing of some people who do. Linguist, musician, performer, communicator, seeker, Haleh is like conduit for the energies that also enlivened Rumi and, through her translations, I can see him: dancing, looking, calling out, whispering, shouting, spinning spinning spinning, praising his friend Shams, honoring Allah with his shouts of joy and lamentations, attending to life and the body and law and struggle with his full attention. A mynah bird has just landed on a branch nearby me. Mimics, they translate too: finding the part of their throats where the sounds they've heard can live through them. This one has gone from ticks to roars to purrs to song in the space of a minute.

5. WHAT'S THE MOST REBELLIOUS THING YOU'VE EVER DONE IN YOUR CREATIVE WORK?

Rebellious according to whom? I have dared many things: to speak about religion and sex and the body as a gay man who has been through reparative therapies and exorcisms. But my guess is that anyone who'd find such writing rebellious isn't interested in hearing what I have to say (if they're even thinking of me; and I suspect they are not). So any rebellions in my creativity were mostly about my own relationship to my own relationship to my self... which, when you put it like that, appears just for what it is: centered on my self. The relationship to self is always going to be a serious relationship, but I hope, like the relationship to whatever God might be, I can look more through that connection, than at. I imagine any audience to my work is also looking at their lives, even anybody who reads my work and doesn't agree with what I do with religion. But their lives are far more interesting than their opinions about me, and I want my imagination of their lives to be one of curiosity, not certitude. I suppose all of this is a way to say that art is more interesting than rebellion. I wrote a sequence of poems where Jesus, Son of God, fresh out of Hell, has a deep dialogue—erotic, frenetic, enraged, centering—with Persephone, queen of destruction, the Daughter of Gods. Someone suggested to me and said I had missed an opportunity for queering Jesus and giving him a male lover (Hermes? Hades? Apollo?).

I could vaguely see what they meant, but art rarely follows a line of a plot: for me, writing an encounter between these two devastated gods was imagination enough. Rebellion for rebellion's sake doesn't interest me any more. I'm interested in imagination and seeing where it takes me.

6. IF YOUR YOUNGER SELF COULD SEE YOU NOW, WHAT WOULD SURPRISE THEM THE MOST? WHAT WOULD DISAPPOINT THEM?

I think about my younger self a lot, but less in terms of surprise or disappointment. Mostly the energy goes back the other way: I have respect for the child and young man who felt like he had no map. He didn't know the way, and to tell anyone about his secrets would have been to make life more difficult. He made it, anyway, or in some kind of way. Bruised, battered, slow. Self confident, strange, self destructive. Making art that knew more than he knew. Filled with self-consciousness, but also with an ambition. The cardinal is back. Maybe it's not a cardinal—its coloring is more varied: butter yellow beak; black around its eyes; red feathers on its underbelly; purple wings. Lively. Sprite. Is it some kind of parrot? Is it a god? Oh the glory of this bird. I have no internet or mobile signal here, and my phone isn't by me anyway, so I am without the ability to record or snap or look for information. The longer I look at it, the less interested I am in its definition anyway: what would information give me other than information? What I have is now, and I cannot stop looking at this bird, who has no interest in me. Perhaps that's what would surprise the younger me: that I'd learn to be unafraid. What would disappoint the younger me? That it would take so much time. What would intrigue the younger me? That it took so much time. There was a green gecko here just five seconds ago. Gone now. I love those little lizards.

7. WHAT IS A TRUTH YOU'VE HAD TO UNLEARN IN ORDER TO GROW?

Fear. God.

8. WHAT QUESTION ARE YOU CURRENTLY TRYING TO ANSWER THROUGH YOUR WORK?

Last night, I was invited by a new friend on Maui, Li, to go to an event in the home of Mary Anna and Steve Grimes, a night of music. I got the impression that many of the musicians there were friends or acquaintances; many of them had clearly known and loved each other for decades. They had stories of adversities overcome, wounds worn and borne, griefs marked. Moana and Keola Beamer played and sang, Keola on the guitar, and Moana singing and summoning up the ancestors by usage of the poi ball, as well as dancing hula while the singing was ongoing. What I am thinking of is not just the richness of their offering, it is also the way both of them could bear the beauty of their offering. It isn't easy to share something so exquisite and not interrupt it with yourself, but they made a communion between listener and singer; singer and listener. Something happened in the space between. Not just between me and them, but between me and me: between me and my past and changing present; between joy and lament; between the dead and the living. I am not seeking any answers in the phenomenon of art; I am trying to be in the event.

9. WHAT IS PULLING YOU FORWARD RIGHT NOW?

I am interested in being drawn inward rather than forward. Time works in many ways, and one of the ways to thrive is to find a way to accept that time is going forward as well as make the time for some kind of travel inward; even if the idea of making time is a fiction, it can—like all fiction—do interesting work in us. My friend Jayne is here for some of the time at the Merwin Conservancy. She's an artist and art therapist, and has spent the mornings collecting leaves and flowers from the pathways of the palm forest. She's pressed them into paper and has made a small book of the shapes. I have another old friend with me too, Meister Eckhart. He died about 700 years ago, and wrote around 100 sermons. One of my favorite lines is where he notices fresh flowers on a grave at a convent. He mentions it in his sermon, praising the sister who made the arrangement of flowers, and commemorated the dead in the days of the living. He thought the human person lived on the hinge point between time and eternity: our days bring us through time, our prayers link us to eternity. Friendships—of all kinds—link me to time.

10. IF YOUR CREATIVE WORK IS A MAP, WHERE DOES IT LEAD?

Maps interest me. They are a way to locate oneself today with the experiences—and point of view—of someone who either went that way before, or proposed some vantage point to make plot lines. I love the Czech poet Miroslav Holub's gorgeous poem "A Brief Reflection on Maps" where a battalion of soldiers, lost in a blizzard in the Alps, found a map and made their treacherous way home. However, the map was not of the Alps, it was of the Pyrenees. If my creative work were a map, it would always lead off it. But it's not a map. It's a strange kind of mine; where to go downward is a way of attending to being present and being lost. The poet David Wagoner said in his magnificent poem "Lost"

> *"The trees ahead and bushes beside you*
> *are not lost. Wherever you are is called* Here
> *and you must treat it as a powerful stranger."*

Among the many pieces of wisdom present in this gorgeous poem that strike today are David's choice of the words "ahead" and "beside" in the first line. One is looking forward, one is just adjacent. His poem is interested in neither of these orientations, but—as far as is possible—in the strange event of the here and now.

The cardinal is back again. On a sturdy twig of a small shrub-like tree. It's peering down, chirping, perhaps looking for something to eat: a worm? a berry?

It's raining lightly, I only see it when I look at the spaces between the trunks closely. And there's a wind through the palm forest that reminds me why in many languages a name for breath is a name for God which is also the sound of what we cannot see. There's sunshine also, glinting on the cartilage of the cardinal's beak. The bird is hungry—or, at least, is seeking something that will sustain it on the edge of living. Me too.

uncharted
with Chris La Tray

ON ROUND DANCES, RESISTANCE, AND THE NIGHT SKY AS GUIDE

Chris La Tray is a Métis storyteller, descended from the Pembina Band of the mighty Red River of the North and a citizen of the Little Shell Tribe of Chippewa Indians. His most recent book, *Becoming Little Shell: A Landless Indian's Journey Home* (Milkweed Editions, 2024), has been widely acclaimed, earning the Pacific Northwest Book Award, the Writing the West Award, and recognition as Best Memoir of the Year by both *People* and *Esquire.*

His debut, *One-Sentence Journal: Short Poems and Essays* from the World at Large, won the 2018 Montana Book Award and a 2019 High Plains Book Award. He followed that with a collection of haiku and haibun poetry, *Descended from a Travel-worn Satchel* (2021).

In addition to his books, Chris has served as the 2025 Kittredge Distinguished Visiting Writer at the University of Montana and received the 2025 Montana Heritage Keeper Award from the Montana Historical Society. He also writes the weekly newsletter *An Irritable Métis.*

Chris lives near Frenchtown, Montana, and was honored to serve as Montana's 11th Poet Laureate from 2023 to 2025.

1. WHAT'S LIGHTING YOU UP CREATIVELY RIGHT NOW?

Reminding people that what we are seeing from our political leaders isn't an anomaly, it's the system operating as it's always been designed to. I think marginalized people understand this because we have had lifetimes of looking over our shoulders but for stunned white, middle class and higher folks—people who never thought they would be touched directly by the shittier aspects of our society—it's something of a moment. It sucks, yeah, but also, what a time for them to actually see the plights of people they have lived side-by-side with but never really saw before. I thought Covid would provide that shakeup but it really hasn't; the status quo returned to business as usual far quicker than I thought it would. Maybe now is the time meaningful societal change moves beyond lip service, but who can say. Convenience is a heady intoxicant. But creative people bear some responsibility to keep what many may see as radical ideas front and center and I'm here for it.

2. WHAT'S THE LAST THING THAT TRULY CAPTIVATED YOU—AN IDEA, A PLACE, A PIECE OF ART, A POEM, A MOMENT?

Last spring I was invited to attend a round dance at my tribe's cultural center. The organizer invited drummers from all over the region—Blackfeet, Cree, Dakota and Nakoda—and when it started, there was a large circle of fourteen young men with hand drums all singing and playing together. The volume and the energy was absolutely thrilling and transcendent. I felt it in every fiber of my body.

3. WHAT'S A RECENT EXPERIENCE THAT MADE YOU FEEL DEEPLY PRESENT?

I was driving through the Bison Range on the CSKT Reservation and had to stop for a buffalo—or *bizhiki,* in Anishinaabemowin—jam. There was a large bull standing on a low rise right next to the road, maybe two arm's lengths away from where I had to coast to a stop. This was early August, deep into the rut, so his tongue was hanging out, and he was breathing hard and grunting, and we just looked at each other face to face, dark eyes to dark eyes. He wasn't showing any signs otherwise of aggression, just interest, and I felt our shared gaze was happening across many swirls of time. It doesn't take much for me to be moved by this older-than-human relative, and this was a particularly profound experience.

THE VOLUME AND THE ENERGY WAS ABSOLUTELY THRILLING AND TRANSCENDENT. I FELT IT IN EVERY FIBER OF MY BODY.

4. WHAT'S A PIECE OF ART, A BOOK, OR A CONVERSATION THAT'S BEEN LIVING IN YOUR MIND RENT-FREE?

Any of the work by Leanne Betasamosake Simpson, whose most recent book is called, *Theory of Water: Nishnaabe Maps to the Times Ahead.* Leanne is a Michi Saagiig Nishnaabeg person of many, many talents, and the boldest of revolutionaries. I'm a deep admirer of her. Next year is the 250th anniversary of the United States, you know, and a couple of my comrades and I are planning to organize a follow-up to an Indigenous storytelling festival called IndigiPalooza MT we just survived with one dedicated to the idea of 250 Years of Resistance... and Counting. I'm hoping to convince Simpson of the worthiness of joining us, even if she is Canadian. After all, we didn't cross the border, the border crossed us!

5. WHAT'S THE MOST REBELLIOUS THING YOU'VE EVER DONE IN YOUR CREATIVE WORK?

Saying no to things I don't want to do. As artists we spend too many years living in scarcity mindset where we are too easily coerced into saying yes to invitations that don't serve us. Saying no to things that seem like no brainers to say yes to, even tiny little things, can be a powerful form of resistance when our survival depends on changing the game.

6. IF YOUR YOUNGER SELF COULD SEE YOU NOW, WHAT WOULD SURPRISE THEM THE MOST? WHAT WOULD DISAPPOINT THEM?

My younger self would be shocked that I ever really started writing poetry, let alone served as the state's poet laureate. As for disappointment? That I still haven't seen Judas Priest live.

7. WHAT IS A TRUTH YOU'VE HAD TO UNLEARN IN ORDER TO GROW?

That when push comes to shove people will do the "right" thing. Just look at what is happening in Gaza and how the vast majority of the global north is reacting to it. It's horrific and we are allowing it to unfold right in front of us with barely more than a pained shrug, let alone general strikes and mayhem in the streets to make a change. I've learned one can be open-hearted and lead with love and still be wary and expect the worst. The hope is to be surprised and I often am or I'd have given up entirely.

8. WHAT QUESTION ARE YOU CURRENTLY TRYING TO ANSWER THROUGH YOUR WORK?

I've thought long and hard about this query and I really don't think there is one. Questions certainly arise but they aren't paddling the canoe.

9. WHAT IS PULLING YOU FORWARD RIGHT NOW?

Cold weather. I love fall and winter and I can hardly wait for them to arrive. The dark time of year is when I feel most alive and it is all just lingering on the near horizon. So long as my heart doesn't give out in the meantime—literally or emotionally—I think I'm going to make it!

10. IF YOUR CREATIVE WORK IS A MAP, WHERE DOES IT LEAD?

Where we're going, we don't need maps. The night sky will tell us all we need to know.

uncharted
with James Crews

ON KINDNESS, CREATIVE REBELLION, AND SAYING YES TO WHAT MATTERS

James Crews (he/him) makes a compelling case for attention, gratitude, and everyday grace. The editor behind the bestselling anthologies *The Path to Kindness: Poems of Connection and Joy* and *How to Love the World: Poems of Gratitude and Hope*, he's been featured in *The Washington Post, The Boston Globe, The New York Times Magazine, The New Republic, The Christian Science Monitor*, and on *NPR's Morning Edition*. Crews is also the author of four prize-winning poetry collections *The Book of What Stays, Telling My Father, Bluebird,* and *Every Waking Moment* as well as the short-essay collection *Kindness Will Save the World: Stories of Compassion and Connection.* When he isn't speaking or leading workshops on kindness, mindfulness, and writing for self-compassion, he's at home with his husband on forty rocky acres in the woods of southern Vermont. In the conversation that follows, Crews reflects on how poems can reorient us toward wonder, connection, and the steadier parts of a difficult world.

1. WHAT'S LIGHTING YOU UP CREATIVELY RIGHT NOW?

What's bringing me alive lately is creative freedom. I always start my days with a large cup of coffee and free-writing in my notebook for a few pages, practicing radical acceptance of whatever wants to come (what Julia Cameron has called "Morning Pages" in *The Artist's Way*). It's easy to fall out of this habit, to forget how important it is to give my heart and mind this kind of free range to explore. Just this morning, I felt lit up again telling the truth about what I love and don't love about my life. And the thing that arose over and over, which has helped me to stay in creative flow, was stability. It's not a very exciting notion for most creatives, but I realize that my daily practice of sitting down at my desk first thing and opening the door to whatever arises has helped me create a strong foundation from which the rest of the day unfolds. I often think of the well-known Ralph Waldo Emerson quote: "A foolish consistency is the hobgoblin of little minds." I've often spurned stability and consistency as too boring and uninspiring. Yet in the last five years, the wise consistency of continually showing up every day to the page, and not seeking out the drama that once marked my life, has brought about more creative abundance than I ever could have hoped for.

2. WHAT'S THE LAST THING THAT TRULY CAPTIVATED YOU— AN IDEA, A PLACE, A PIECE OF ART, A POEM, A MOMENT?

I have written elsewhere that "only moments matter," and this is one of the mantras I try to live by. Both of my parents died quite young—my father at 43 years old, from complications of Hepatitis C, and my mother at 64 from sudden heart failure. Spending time with them in their final months and days showed me over and over that the so-called smallest moments are the ones that stay with us the most. The moment that sprang to mind when I first read this question may not seem all that earth-shattering or relevant, but I have carried it with me for weeks now. My husband Brad and I were walking a piece of land here in Vermont, where we're trying to find a place to create a farm and retreat center. It was the perfect summer day, and we pulled over on a mostly deserted road to walk the unmown fields of the property. I'd been overly busy, and felt a little resentful that I'd taken time away from my packed schedule to drive the hour there and back. Yet as soon as we began to step through Queen Anne's lace and goldenrod, a sudden sense of peace fell over me. I looked down to see a black swallowtail butterfly nectaring on a pink clover flower, and seemed to feel my soul at last rising to the surface again, just in this single moment of close attention. Ultimately, that piece of land didn't end up being right for us, but that bit of what Anne Lamott has called "soul time" continues to stay with me, a reminder of what's most essential, the space I need in my life through which to cultivate a sense of wonder. It's as if watching that butterfly flex its wings and drink showed me again how I might nourish myself, spending time away from work, distraction, and news.

3. WHAT'S A RECENT EXPERIENCE THAT MADE YOU FEEL DEEPLY PRESENT?

I always feel most present when I am immersed in a poem or essay, or when I'm listening and responding to someone else's work. I host a monthly writing community on Zoom called *The Monthly Pause*, and just a few days ago, I found all of my worries and fatigue falling away from me as I listened deeply and generously to what folks had written during our time together. I believe this practice of receiving, even living inside a piece that someone has created, makes me a better writer myself. I stay alert for phrases and lines that stand out to me, and reflect that back to the writer, focusing on what draws my attention. I do the same in my own work too, especially during the revision process. No doubt, this kind of generous listening seeps into daily life as well, making me more attentive, more alert to inspiration whenever and however it slips into me.

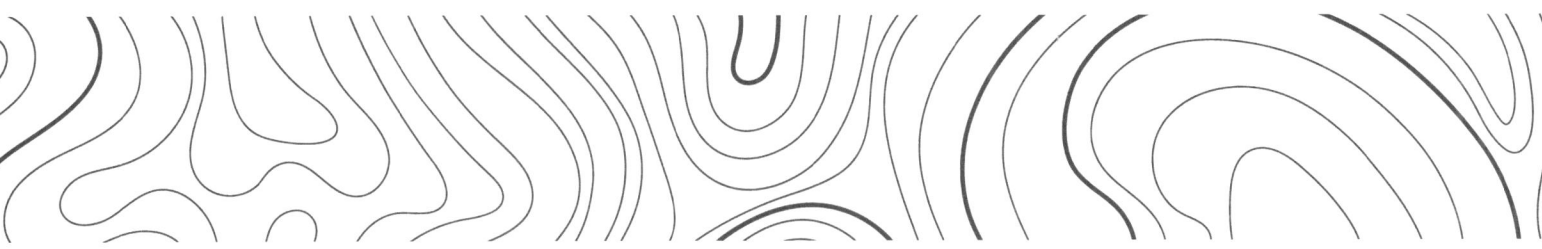

4. WHAT'S A PIECE OF ART, A BOOK, OR A CONVERSATION THAT'S BEEN LIVING IN YOUR MIND RENT-FREE?

My best friend, whom I have known for 25 years now, recently visited me. As we walked through a local nature preserve, she confessed that she's been struggling to stay present to where she lives, and to the work she's doing right now. She foresees a move down the road eventually, but doesn't want to just reject her daily experience, missing out on what's actually there to appreciate. Lately, she said, she's been seeing each new day as the perfect tangerine, round and fragrant and filled with its own particular sugars. It's up to us whether or not we choose to feast on the tangerine of each given day, whether we even start to peel it, or decide to leave it untouched. Needless to say, this conversation has stayed with me, and has made me even more present to the gift of a new day, even when there are parts of my life I'd rather reject.

5. WHAT'S THE MOST REBELLIOUS THING YOU'VE EVER DONE IN YOUR CREATIVE WORK?

One of the bravest things I ever did was publish my first anthology of poems focused on kindness, *Healing the Divide*. This was an act of rebellion for me not only because of the theme, but also because I gathered only accessible poems that spoke to a larger, more mainstream audience. I was teaching beginning creative writing at SUNY-Albany at the time, and the idea came to me following the 2016 election. The students in my classes came from diverse backgrounds, many of them from in and around New York City, and I could tell that, given the rhetoric and actions of our government, they were losing hope in humanity. Poetry has always been the lens through which I see and process the world, and so I thought it would be helpful to put together a book that might give them more faith in the future. The book I eventually published would go on to reach far more people than I ever could have dreamed, but I'll never forget returning to Lincoln, Nebraska, where I had done my PhD, for a reading. One of my former classmates was commenting on the collection, and I told him how surprised I was by its success. "Well," he said with a discernible sneer. "It's not all that surprising. Target sells T-shirts with the word 'kindness' printed on them." I could feel the sting of those words, meant to belittle the book and its accomplishments. But having been on a reading tour for the anthology, and seen how my own students and many other readers connected with these poems, I knew that, no matter what anyone else thought, this book would touch many lives, and give poetry a wider audience. I remain proud to this day that I said a difficult "yes" to this departure from the more "literary" projects I was trained by academia to pursue.

6. IF YOUR YOUNGER SELF COULD SEE YOU NOW, WHAT WOULD SURPRISE THEM THE MOST? WHAT WOULD DISAPPOINT THEM?

If my younger self could see me now, he would be shocked that I make my living speaking to large groups, leading workshops and retreats, publishing books. I first came to poetry in the third grade when my teacher Mrs. Brown required us to memorize and recite a poem to the whole class each week for a unit in our English class. I don't even know where the thought first came from, but one week I found myself standing at her desk, turning five different shades of red as I asked her if I could write, memorize and recite one of my own poems. She clapped her hands, excited by the idea, and I became a writer in that instant. After I shared my poem, people came up to me—the quietest kid in class—and complimented what I had written, saying they couldn't believe that came from me. It felt like a miracle, that something I had created out of nothing, sparked a reaction like this in people who had never even spoken to me. Since then, I knew I wanted to write, wanted to share my work, but I never thought I would be fortunate enough to do it as part of my job. I also never thought one could be both introverted and still comfortable enough speaking to large audiences. In spite of all this, I think my younger self would be disappointed that I sometimes lose myself too much in the business of "adulting," and often stray from the wonder and awe that brought me to writing in the first place. This is something I'm working on right now, allowing myself what feels like an indulgent amount of time some days to "do nothing," just walking or sitting in the garden, exploring a town I've never been to, sitting at a cafe for hours without the armor of my laptop and a task to do. This type of spaciousness feels necessary to my creativity. Yet the older I get, the more rare it seems, the easier it becomes to make excuses to avoid it.

7. WHAT IS A TRUTH YOU'VE HAD TO UNLEARN IN ORDER TO GROW?

One so-called "truth" I've had to unlearn is that an artist has to suffer in order to create their work. Because of our grind culture, and the myths surrounding creativity, I believed that if it felt too easy, it wasn't worth doing. I've always worked hard, but I thought that writing should feel difficult, that I wasn't living up to my potential somehow if I wasn't struggling. I grew up in a very chaotic home where my father was often switching jobs, and we moved every few years, often falling behind in the rent. My mother also lived with agoraphobia and other mental illnesses, so stability was hard to come by. We never knew when she might have another panic attack, or when we'd have to move suddenly from a beloved house. I think I got addicted to constant movement and drama, and carried that over into my adult life and writing practice. In therapy over the years, and in my marriage with my husband, I've worked to unravel this addiction, and to embrace the fact that one can be a happy and productive artist—without all the drama. I've learned to follow what feels good, what flows more easily through my writing.

8. WHAT QUESTION ARE YOU CURRENTLY TRYING TO ANSWER THROUGH YOUR WORK?

I lost my mother a few years ago. She had been ill for many years with multiple sclerosis and COPD, and I'd acted as her caregiver for most of my life. But her death came as a shock to my system, leaving me without a sense of equilibrium or purpose. I realize, looking back, that I took her for granted, even with the awareness that she was not well, and even given the fact that I had lost my father 20 years before. The recent death of Andrea Gibson, a poet who influenced my own work profoundly over the past few years, reopened this wound, and has me asking this question in my poetry and essays: *How can I live close to death, and welcome the braided nature of sorrow and joy into my daily life, without also dwelling in anxiety and fear? In other words: How can I live without taking anyone or anything for granted?*

One thing that's been helping in this quest is a quote from Andrea: "Remind me/all my prayers were answered/the moment I started praying/for what I already have." To me, this speaks to our constant human dilemma, of how to radically appreciate what is right here in front of us, even in the midst of sorrow, even with life's inherent imperfections and failures. Their quote also speaks to the realization that, when and if circumstances shift, we might ask for this very imperfect and beautiful life we spend so much time trying to escape. Most likely, someday, we will want it back.

9. WHAT IS PULLING YOU FORWARD RIGHT NOW?

Honestly, some days not much pulls me forward. My heart breaks constantly for the ways in which our country has been overtaken by casual cruelty, the ways our government is ignoring the genocide in Gaza, the attacks on LGBTQ+ people, people of color, and vulnerable groups everywhere. It is very easy to lose hope in the face of such violent rhetoric and outright lies. One thing that buoys me is finding a sense of purpose, both in writing every day and sharing my work with others. My husband and I recently edited a book of love poems by LGBTQ+ authors and allies called Love Is for All of Us, and being out on tour for that anthology, traveling all over the country and visiting bookstores in many different communities, renewed our spirits. Gathering in the name of something larger than us as individuals—love, tenderness, and belonging—helped us and everyone who came to our readings tap into a deeper well of energy. I try to be very intentional with the work I create and put into the world.

I want the poems, essays, and anthologies I share to help make our planet a kinder, more beautiful place. I also recently interviewed the singer/songwriter and poet Carrie Newcomer for my writing community, asking a similar question: What's keeping you going at this fraught time? She replied simply, "Leaning into beauty." When I heard her words, I felt an opening up of permission in my body and in myself to do the same. Right now, I'm watching endangered monarch butterflies, bumblebees, and hummingbird moths feed on the purple blossoms of butterfly bushes we have allowed to grow wild in our backyard. Small moments of beauty, and small kindnesses I offer and receive—what the awe researcher Dacher Keltner calls "moral beauty"—all help pull me forward on the best days. And remembering that they are possible on my worst days helps me look ahead to better times.

10. IF YOUR CREATIVE WORK IS A MAP, WHERE DOES IT LEAD?

If my creative work is a map, I think it leads to more mystery. The more I practice writing and other forms of creativity, the less I feel I know. For a long time, I think I thought the map would lead to success, fame, or a teaching position as a professor—but it has only led me more deeply into myself and my own experience, more deeply into the mysteries that govern our existence. I was once lucky enough to take a weeklong workshop with the poet Li-Young Lee, and I'll never forget what he said: "Writing is a self-clarifying act." As we move through the layers of self, however, we keep finding more layers. More and more lately, I seem to have left behind all maps, and now feel guided by Something I don't quite understand, but which feels both present and real. I retrieve and receive more than I believe I actually create. I don't mean to say that I don't still strive, but it feels more like an act of service to what the poem, essay, or book wants to be, rather than what I want it to be. More often, I am trying softer instead of harder. If my creative work is a map at all, I suppose it's one of those complex, nearly indecipherable subway maps with countless stops on the journey—but with no discernible destination. At one point, this might have felt frightening to me, but what a joy it still is to ride this train, getting on and getting off where it feels right, not needing to know where I'm headed anymore.

HOW CAN I LIVE CLOSE TO DEATH, AND WELCOME THE BRAIDED NATURE OF SORROW AND JOY INTO MY DAILY LIFE, WITHOUT ALSO DWELLING IN ANXIETY AND FEAR? IN OTHER WORDS: HOW CAN I LIVE WITHOUT TAKING ANYONE OR ANYTHING FOR GRANTED?

uncharted
with Ana Maria Spagna

ON ECOLOGY, QUEERNESS, AND THE PRACTICE OF UNKNOWING

Ana Maria Spagna (she/her) has spent a life at the intersection of wild places and human stories. Raised in Riverside, California and long rooted in the North Cascades, she's the author of nine books on nature, work, community, and history—most recently *Pushed: Miners, a Merchant and (Maybe) a Massacre*, her investigation into xenophobia in the Inland Northwest. Her essays have appeared in *Orion, Sierra, Ecotone, Fourth Genre, Creative Nonfiction, Brevity, The Normal School,* and *High Country News*, and her work has been recognized by the Society for Environmental Journalists, the Pacific Northwest Booksellers Association, and as a four-time finalist for the Washington State Book Award. Before turning to teaching in low-residency MFA programs at Antioch University Los Angeles and Western Colorado University (and in visiting roles at Whitman College, the University of Montana, St. Lawrence University, and Wenatchee Valley College) Spagna spent fifteen years on backcountry trail crews for the National Park Service. She now lives with her wife, Laurie, in Stehekin, Washington, a remote community accessible only by foot or ferry. In the conversation that follows, Spagna reflects on ecology, Queerness, and the stories we inherit and those we choose to tell.

I. WHAT'S LIGHTING YOU UP CREATIVELY RIGHT NOW?

I am intrigued and inspired by ways to write about our relationships with the more-than-human world. These relationships seem as rich and complex as human relationships and caught up with human relationships, and I love thinking about how to capture this complexity. I wrote an essay last fall for *Brevity* magazine making use of the pronouns "ki" and "kin" for both human and non-human characters, as suggested by Robin Wall Kimmerer in her essay "Nature Needs a New Pronoun." I also wrote about queerness and fear and rattlesnakes in an essay for *LA Review* that was inspired, in part, by Nikki Giovanni's poem "Allowables."

2. WHAT'S THE LAST THING THAT TRULY CAPTIVATED YOU—AN IDEA, A PLACE, A PIECE OF ART, A POEM, A MOMENT?

3. WHAT'S A RECENT EXPERIENCE THAT MADE YOU FEEL DEEPLY PRESENT?

The answer to these are one in the same. On a road trip through the West, after a long day in the car, a friend and I stumbled on a free Afro-pop outdoor concert in downtown Boise, Idaho. Kids and dogs frolicked in foundations. Adults danced. The sun played on office buildings not a half mile from a river where families floated in intertubes. The whole scene reminded me of the joy of summer and the joy of community.

4. WHAT'S A PIECE OF ART, A BOOK, OR A CONVERSATION THAT'S BEEN LIVING IN YOUR MIND RENT-FREE?

So many! CMarie Fuhrman's essay collection, *Salmon Weather.* The novel *Stone Yard Devotional* by Charlotte Wood. The music of Hooray for the Riff Raff. I saw them live and could not get over the energy!

5. WHAT'S THE MOST REBELLIOUS THING YOU'VE EVER DONE IN YOUR CREATIVE WORK?

I think using "ki" and "kin" was pretty rebellious. I also think the stubborn insistence on including my queerness in my essays for the last 25 years has been a kind of rebellion. It doesn't seem so today, but I remember one of the first reviewers of my first essay collection said something like "I don't know why those people always have to write about their sexuality." Which, of course, made me double down.

6. IF YOUR YOUNGER SELF COULD SEE YOU NOW, WHAT WOULD SURPRISE THEM THE MOST? WHAT WOULD DISAPPOINT THEM?

I suppose it's a tie between my many years running a chainsaw, an ambition young Ana Maria couldn't have imagined, and my many published books, an ambition young Ana Maria certainly held ... but probably didn't believe possible. She'd be disappointed that I'm a teacher now. My mother was a teacher, and kids never want to become their parents, though I'm quite proud to follow in her footsteps now.

WHAT DO WE OWE OUR MORE-THAN-HUMAN KIN? HOW CAN WE RIGHTLY HONOR THEM, EVEN AS WE WORK TO HONOR HUMANS WHO ARE OTHERED FOR WHATEVER REASON.

7. WHAT IS A TRUTH YOU'VE HAD TO UNLEARN IN ORDER TO GROW?

I used to think you used to have to be an expert before you began to write about a topic. Now I'm embracing "unknowing" as not only a starting point but a sharing point.

8. WHAT QUESTION ARE YOU CURRENTLY TRYING TO ANSWER THROUGH YOUR WORK?

What do we owe our more-than-human kin? How can we rightly honor them, even as we work to honor humans who are *othered* for whatever reason.

9. WHAT IS PULLING YOU FORWARD RIGHT NOW?

The kinship of humans and more-than-humans on the day to day.

10. IF YOUR CREATIVE WORK IS A MAP, WHERE DOES IT LEAD?

Outside. Full stop.

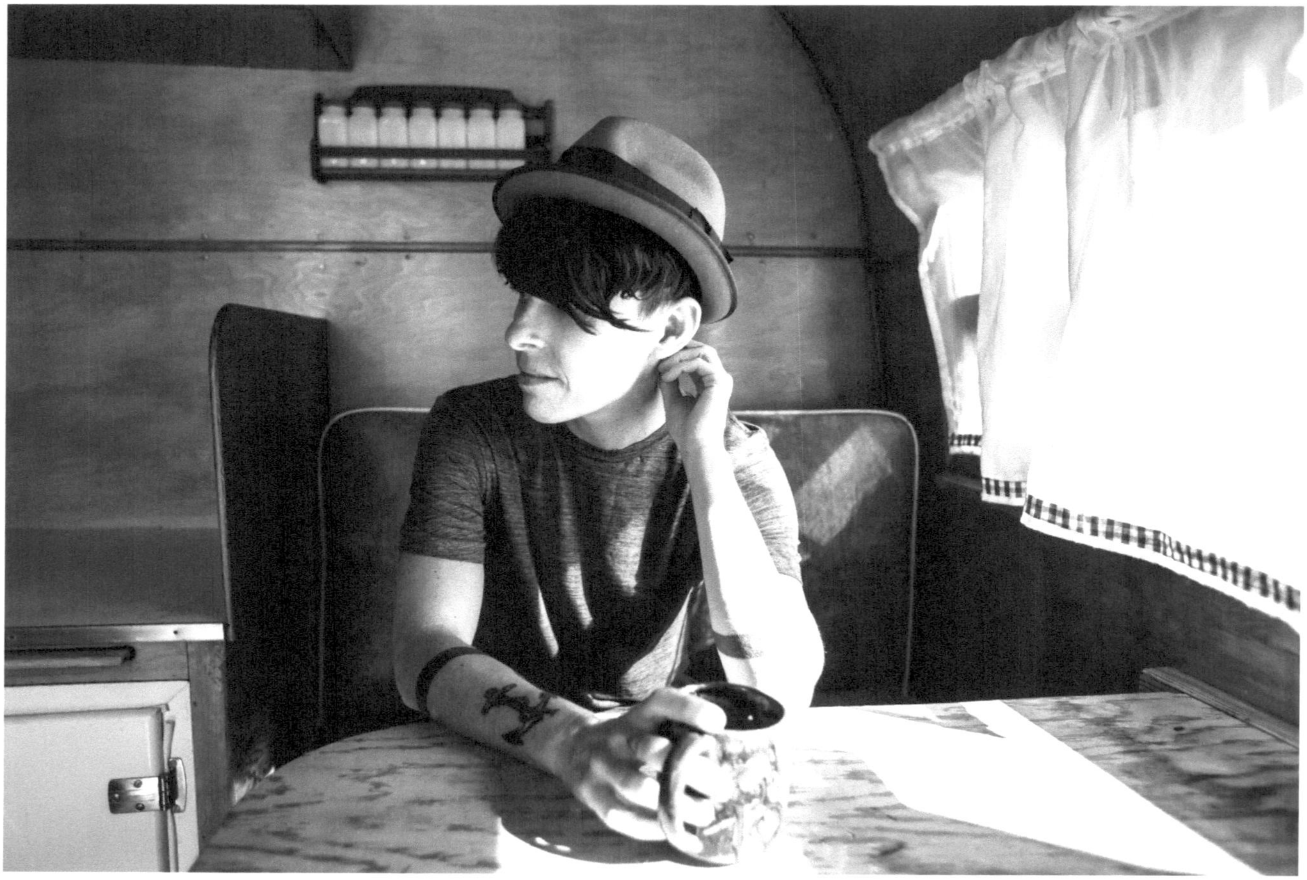

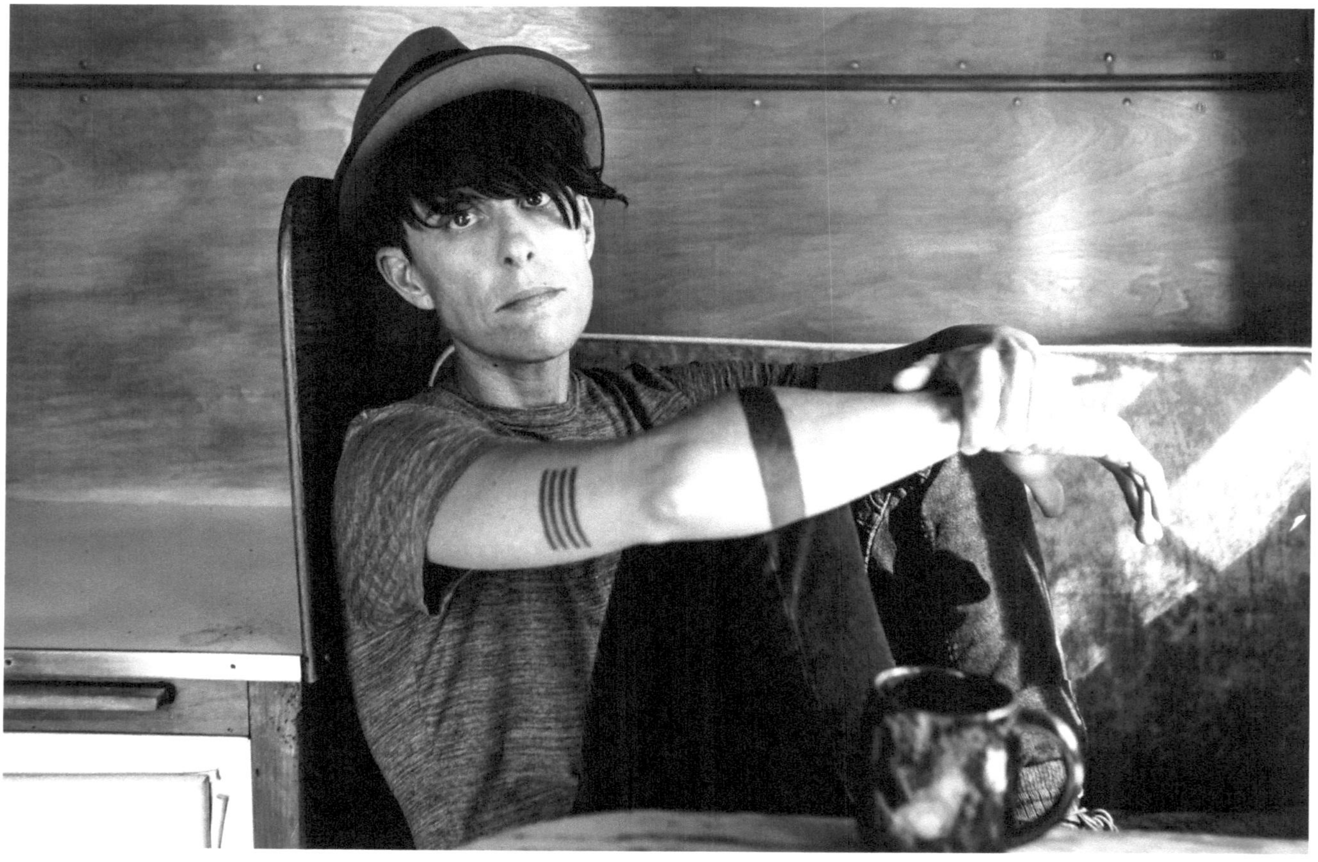

Our Angel of the Get Through

AN INTERVIEW WITH ANDREA GIBSON

*Shared from the Wayfarer (2018) archive in memory of
Gibson's life and passing August 13, 1975 – July 14, 2025*

I first saw Andrea Gibson (they/them) perform during their *Hey Galaxy* tour at Babefest
(a feminist-focused festival) in Provincetown, MA. The headliner was Ani DiFranco. I remember
sitting in my seat in the intimate theater waiting for DiFranco to come out when I read that
Andrea Gibson would be the opening voice. I remember thinking to myself how odd it was for a
poet to be the opening act for a musician. As a poet myself, I don't say this with judgment but
rather with curiosity. When Gibson took the stage and began reciting their poetry, everything
became clear.

The poem recited: *Orlando* (touching on the Orlando shooting, which had happened only
months before). There is little I can do to convey how powerful this poem is other than to say, in
my humble opinion, that night the opening voice was even more captivating than the headliner,
so instead I will simply encourage you to look up Gibson on YouTube, watch *Orlando* and listen
to it and then purchase it on iTunes so you can revisit it again. Gibson's most notable accolades
being Four-time Denver Grand Slam Champion and Women of the World Poetry Slam champion
2008. Born in Calais, Maine, Gibson has lived in Boulder Colorado since 1999. Their poetry and
activism primarily center on gender norms, politics, social reform, and the struggles LGBTQIA+
people face in today's society

Connor: I'm going to dive right in. After seeing your first open-mic in Denver in 2000, you felt inspired to become a spoken word artist. What took place internally while you watched that open mic? What resonated so deeply with you?

Andrea: I attended my first open mic in Boulder, CO, and my first poetry slam a few weeks later in Denver. I had written throughout my life but had such overwhelming stage fright I never imagined I would ever willingly read my poems aloud in front of an audience. Looking back now I realize that much of what drew me to the stage was how afraid I was of it. Fortunately (ha!) for me that fear has hardly subsided in 19 years of performing. My experience of attending poetry events these days is not very different than it was in the beginning. I don't know if it's possible to faint from goosebumps, but I feel on the verge of that consistently when listening to spoken word.

In *Lord of the Butterflies* you write, "Your name is a gift, you can return if it doesn't fit." In addition to "Andrea," you've also chosen the name "Andrew" and use gender-neutral pronouns, (specifically they/them/theirs). What were some of the mile-marker realizations along your process of defining yourself on the gender spectrum?

I was in touch with my gender long before I came to terms with my sexuality, and long before I had language to define myself. As a child I very simply didn't feel like a boy or a girl, and doubted I would ever grow up to feel like a woman or a man. In 2004 I heard the word "genderqueer" for the first time and immediately thought, "YES!" It wasn't until quite a few years later though that I started asking my intimate community to use non-binary (they/them/theirs) pronouns for me, and a couple of years later I began using them publicly and writing more consistently about my own gender journey. In regards to my name—I don't have much personal attachment to one, OR—maybe I just like having many names. Someone could ask 10 of my friends what they call me and there would be 10 different answers—Andrea, Andrew, Dre, Giba, Faye, Gib, Gibby, Sam, Andy, Pangee, Buttercup— yeah, I actually have a friend who calls me Buttercup. :)

Ha. That is amazing! We should all have that friend. As someone who struggles with mental Illness, I see your own struggles with anxiety, depression, self-esteem, shame—all these inner-dynamics—run like veins throughout your body of work. As one who likewise struggles with depression, cPTSD and shame, one of the most-resonate lines for me is: "I think the hardest people in the world to forgive are the people we once were."

The unabashed authenticity with which you approach the pen unites all of us outliers, letting us know we are not alone. When did you decide that you were going to share those aspects of yourself? Was it a conscious choice to enter into this dialogue so wrought with taboo or were you simply being yourself?

People create their safety in different ways. I have a few friends who feel most safe when what they are experiencing internally is something they process internally. I'm the opposite. The more I share about what's happening in my emotional world, the more the tornado of my nervous system settles down. I don't doubt that that has been, in many ways, a response to trauma—my historical desire to have a voice that is heard, but it's one I feel good about honoring regardless. That said, as I've grown older, and have learned more and more to be the one who listens to myself, the one who shows up with softness when something deep inside of me starts screaming, I have less of a need to write to be heard as an individual, and more of a desire to show up creatively to a world harmed by silence. As you touch on above—there is so much we have in common, and reminders that we are not alone can be life saving. Those reminders have certainly saved my life many many times.

When you recite a poem, your voice reverts with rhythmic, raging, raw rhymes. Each time you perform, you seem to not be reciting the poem but living it. When I gave a TED Talk on my own reality with mental illness, I felt like a streaker on stage—naked—only it was being recorded for posterity. The level of vulnerability was both terrifying and transcendent. Do you find it emotionally draining to give so much of yourself in every book, every performance? How do you refill yourself?

I most often find writing and performing energizing. I feel more alive while doing both than I do at almost any other time in my life lately. But there are some poems and some topics that leave me feeling more naked than others. For example, I have chronic Lyme disease, and speaking to that on stage specifically is something that I can't always do. When I started diving into the why of that I soon recognized that it's, in large part, because of the tenderness of my audiences. I feel most vulnerable when I can feel people worrying about me and when I speak to my health (what I perceive as) worry sometimes permeates the room. It's one of the places where I've been calling myself to be braver and to show up more courageously to my discomfort.

In *Angels of the Get-Through,* you write, "I am already building the museum / For every treasure you unearth in the rock bottom / Holy vulnerable cliff God mason, heart heavier than all the bricks Say this is what the pain made of you / An open open open road An avalanche of feel it all / Don't ever let anyone tell you, you are too much / Or it has been too long" Is your creative process an excavation of rock-bottom? Is it the alchemy of transcending this life's pains into something of beauty? From what mental place do you usually take up the pen?

When I look at my life I don't see many absolute facts. Nor do I see many absolute truths. My life is what I call it and the more I have called it beautiful the more beautiful it has become. What I have called my biggest wounds have very often been my biggest blessings, because of where they

led me, and because of how often they further opened my heart. I don't want to say any of this flippantly and without respect for how real this hurting world's walls are in relation to how possible it is to see the light in any given moment. But I have needed, for my own sanity, to find that light in every instant I possibly could, and that is most often where I write from, though it is not the only place. ...I'll say one of the other primary places I speak from is rooted in the belief that even when the truth isn't hopeful the telling of it is.

Have you ever written a poem that you were afraid to share? ...have you ever said to yourself, no, this is too intimate; I don't think I can share this one?

Yes. But there was a "yet" on the end of the sentence. "I don't think I can share this one yet." And hopefully soon, I will.

Finally, the first time I saw you perform was at Babefest in Provincetown. You opened for Ani DiFranco. I remember sitting in the audience awestruck as you performed "Orlando" –brought to tears as you kept going, verse by verse, striking the chords of my soul with each word. "People outside pushing bandannas into bullet wounds. It's true, what they say about the gays being so fashionable. Their ghosts never go out of style. Even life, it's like funeral practice. Half of us are already dead to our families before we die. Half of us on our knees trying to crawl into the family photo" What do you view the role of the poet/artist to be in the current political climate?

To inspire an untamable sense of urgency in regards to active boot-laced compassion. To actively imagine a better world and to write it down so that others might imagine it as well. To destroy the myth of our collective powerlessness. To create beauty where there isn't yet beauty. To remind people they are not alone. To un-war our relationships to each other and ourselves.

Solastalgia

AN ESSAY BY EDITOR, FRANCESCA G. VARELA

We walk up the steep gravel trail, breathing in the pungent sunflower-smell of subalpine meadows. Checker-winged dragonflies click past our ears, landing briefly on yellow arnicas and lantern-flowered lupines, rocking the plants by their stems, just as the wind does.

The air feels thinner here at 5,000 feet, and my breath comes heavy as I trudge uphill with a twenty-pound backpack digging into my shoulders. With each step, I swat away clouds of tiny black flies that bite incessantly at my arms and legs, drawn to the salt in my sweat.

There will be many more miles of this before we get to our campsite. It's a long and uphill hike, but it'll be more than worth it. In addition to the magnificent wildflowers, this trail promises up-close views of the tallest mountain in Oregon— Mt. Hood.

I've lived alongside Mt. Hood all my life. I grew up in a suburb of Portland, and, although you couldn't see the mountain from our house, you could see it if you walked a little ways down the street. On sunny days the mountain was there, waiting on the horizon; far off, blue, pale; a towering, intangible, magnificent god.

To me, Mt. Hood has always been "the mountain," just as the Willamette has always been "the river," because I know them best. But there are certainly other mountains nearby. On sterling clear days, you can see the ghostly cap of Mt. Rainier, over 100 miles away, or Mt. Adams, or the flat-topped outline of Mt. St. Helens, which blew its top off in 1980. Mt. Hood is also an active volcano, but, lucky for our backpacking expedition, it hasn't erupted since the 1700s, and it doesn't show signs of doing so any time soon.

The trail takes us uphill and then down again. At last we turn a corner, and there it is, the mountain, almost within touching distance, taking up half the sky. We're so close I can see the beds of gravel that make up its slopes; the bouldered pieces of its body; the brown-gray buttresses that form its silhouette. Mt. Hood.

I feel a pang of something in my stomach. A sadness; a feeling of guilt, of concern, because the mountain looks so much more bare up close—half of it almost completely snowless. It's even worse than I thought.

When I was growing up, Mt. Hood stayed white year-round. Sure, it lost some of its snow in the summer, showing a few cracks in the snowpack, maybe a few rivulets of blue, but nothing like this. Over the past few summers, Mt. Hood has lost more and more of its snow. Now, in early July, it looks purple, almost gray, its strange, ghostly, long-buried skin exposed to the sunlight.

Some of its power is gone. It is no longer an immutable god. Instead, it is fragile. It is lava stone and wind-sculpted cliffs, carved down by rain and weather. The remaining snow lies in dredges, surviving in patches of rock shaded from the sun.

It's climate change. That's what it is. Warmer temperatures mean shorter winters, which mean declining snowpack levels. In spring, the snow and ice melt too quickly, flooding the rivers early in the season rather than melting in small increments throughout the summer. This leads to droughts for glacier-fed rivers and streams during the hottest months of the year,

affecting our drinking water, our communities—our entire ecosystem.

And things are only getting worse. A terrifying study predicts that Mt. Hood won't have enough snow to ski on by 2050. Another study predicts that the entire Cascade Range—which stretches from Northern California to Southern British Columbia—will no longer have any snowpack by 2070. The world is dying, it seems, and we are here, in it, feeling it, experiencing it.

I turn my focus back to the trail. We continue hiking, keeping the mountain to our right as we walk up switchback trails, up and up and up, until we're looking down on canopies of fir and hemlock, and great hillsides padded with lichen and fern. We stand along the cliff and look out across the valley. We can see the hump of Mt. Jefferson and the flat, glimmering edge of the Columbia River. As we rise toward the alpine zone, the trees thin out and shrink, and we pass a few banks of snow, streaked with dirt and boot prints and pine needles, and the grasses grow thick with avalanche lilies and beargrass, and bright red paintbrush flowers. The mountain hangs there behind everything, still beautiful but also a reminder of something—of change. Of sadness. Of loss.

Solastalgia—that's what it is. The sense of sorrow that comes from witnessing the long, slow loss or destruction of a place you love. In this case, the destruction is caused by climate change, a force already in motion, something that cannot be healed, at least not anytime soon. At best, our future could be made less catastrophic, but it can't be fixed, and there is a yearning that comes with that—for control, or perhaps for a return to better times; a sense of nostalgia for something I've never experienced, for a world that is okay, that is healthy, that is not on the brink of ecological collapse. I want to look at the mountains and the forests and to feel only joy and connection, rather than this mix of sadness and love and longing and despair and happiness and anger, this moving tempest of belonging and grief.

By the time we make it to our campsite, the sun is low; late afternoon. We set up our tents at the edge of the world, beneath the open sky. The mountain is already turning to dusk behind us. We replenish our water from a glacial stream, our fingers numb after submerging the bottles for just seconds. Nothing has ever tasted better.

We relax at camp, brushing away ants and flies and mosquitoes, sitting on boulders that were once volcanic ash. The sun sets slowly, sinking into the felted mountain folds, the sky striating into silver, red, purple, pink; into a shade of blue-green that is the same color as spruce needles. A raven flies past us at eye level, because we are up there, raven-high, turkey-vulture-high, cliff-swallow-high, so high that some of the clouds are below us. And we look down like the mountain does; down at the choked sea of cars and homes and roads, at the skyscrapers, so large and blinding that we can see them from sixty miles away; at the freeways, the streetlights, the neon Montgomery Park sign in the industrial cusp of Northwest Portland; at the bridges, snake-like and winding.

When the sun rests flat against the Coast Range, the final things to go dark around us are the beargrass flowers and the mountain itself, dying, there, its long, slow death, the last of its glaciers glistening.

Francesca Varela (she/her) is an environmental writer, freelance copy editor, and award-winning eco-fiction author based in Portland, Oregon. She holds an M.A. in environmental humanities from the University of Utah where she focused her studies on sustainable food systems, environmental justice, and climate change. You can learn more about her work by visiting her website at francescavarela.com!

BECOMING OF VULTURES

AN ESSAY BY CHRIS ROBEY

I had just arrived at my new psychiatrist's office for my intake appointment. I pulled into the parking lot and, after scanning briefly for an open spot, steered toward a large black pickup parked at the edge of the lot where it faced a ribbon of woods. As I pulled up next to the truck, something perched on the driver-side mirror caught my eye. At first I thought it was a raptor-shaped decoy or some other ornament. It was just days away from Halloween, and the truck's owner could have given themselves over to the spirit of the season. My heart leapt when the thing jerked its head slantwise and peered at me with an eye like a bead of India ink. Its face was like a rotten Osage orange. I was being regarded by a black vulture.

I parked, got out, and slowly approached the front of the truck. The vulture continued peering at me over the hood. When I reached the other side, a burst of movement in the grass jostled me again. Not just one but an entire committee of vultures had gathered at the brushy edge of the woods, eight or nine in all. They recollected themselves, some slowly backing into the brush, others bobbing their heads and shrugging their woolly shoulders, all staring me down with the same glimmering eyes as their companion.

A voice from behind broke the deadlock. "Excuse me?"

I turned to see a woman in marine fatigues, boots, and a tight bun approaching.

"I'm so sorry to ask this of you, but would you mind shooing them off?" she said, fingering her key fob. "They freak me out."

I agreed and did so gently. The vultures rustled again but otherwise quietly withdrew into the brush. The ringleader fluttered down from its roost and joined the throng.

The woman stepped closer once the vultures were gone. "Thanks, so sorry to keep you!" she said.

I told her it was no problem at all and started toward the entrance to the office building. As I passed by the passenger door of the pickup, it cracked open to reveal another woman who peered out toward where the committee had gathered. She had been sitting inside the truck the whole time, eyeing the lead vulture warily just as it had been regarding her.

It makes sense that someone like the first woman—presumably a service member who had witnessed or precipitated violent death or likely would one day—should be fearful of vultures. As for the rest of us, what is it about them that elicits such revulsion? That the business of scavenging carcasses is grisly and odorous is a given, and we generally do not like reminders of our mortality. There's also a reminder of our inescapable animal-ness in the way their bodily functions are so unabashedly and prominently on display—they squabble, gorge themselves, projectile vomit when startled, and soil themselves to stay cool.

Human babies do many of these things, too. How is it, then, that when met with other displays of bodily reality we shy away, shoo them off, or meet them with displays of force?

Putting aside the fact that he was a scheming, boastful bigot who mostly killed what he loved, there are parts of John J. Audubon's entry on black vultures in *Birds of America* that I am quite taken with. I do, however, think he lingers too much on the qualities that relegate vultures to the untouchables of the avian world. Still, his observations are important because they reflect how most Americans continue to regard vultures; namely, as carrion crows, haunting meat markets, keeping company with feral dogs, casting shadows over the slaughterhouse, painting their roosts with ordure, tainting cistern water, stalking carts of offal on their way to landfills at the city's edge, grunting, hissing, and gobbling up all manner of ripe flesh. He comments on the force with which they disgorge their stomach's contents with a kind of wonder, and also notes their characteristic obstinateness. Upon approaching a two-acre roost host to thousands in the swamps outside Charleston, he and a companion "kept up a brisk fusillade for several minutes," killing an unspecified number. Those that survived the volley began reconvening in the same trees soon after the gunmen retired for the night.

I just recently learned of how the people of Bunn, North Carolina—a small town 30 miles northeast of Raleigh—have been "besieged" by a "plague" of vultures since 2020. When all else failed, they resorted to using cannon fire to scare the birds off. The apparatus employed is actually fascinating—a propane-fueled sound cannon installed on the roof of the local high school and electronically programmed to fire every day in the morning, afternoon, and evening for two weeks straight. Each blast reaches upwards of 130 decibels and sounds like a skeet shooter with an itchy trigger finger. They are not harmful, ostensibly, and are admittedly a more humane solution than Audubon's habit of disgorging the contents of his

gun. Even so, there is something to be said for making it illegal to kill or maim vultures while sanctioning contraptions that shave a year or two off their lifespans. The use of less-than-lethal weapons on protesters is questionable enough. Their use on animals strikes me with the same bluster as North Korea's missile tests or parents screaming at school board meetings. Both are tactics of riot police. And while it worked for a time, the vultures of Bunn just as soon resumed their posts.

I have wondered if the vultures circling the fields of Antietam made Lincoln reconsider his invocation of "the better angels of our nature." By other ways of reckoning, however, vultures are those better angels. Ancient Zoroastrians and modern-day Parsis maintain that it is by the vulture's mystic eye—so adept at spotting carrion when airborne—that souls are ferried into the afterlife. The diameter of the *dakhma,* or "Towers of Silence," is set to be no smaller than 300 feet—room enough for vultures to take off and land as they fulfill their role in purifying the dead. A similar premise is enacted through the Tibetan practice of *jhator,* or "scattering to the birds." One's body is given up in a final act of charity. Blessed deconstitution, the surrendering of material form to the economy of being.

One of my favorite poems is William Cullen Bryant's "Thanatopsis." The poem reaches well beyond the currents in

19th-century Romanticism it's typically confined to and stands out to me now for the way it speaks to how vultures can be both deathly omens and visiting angels. When Bryant urges us to go forth under the open sky to receive Nature's teachings and elegizes the surrender of our individual beings to the elements, I cannot help but think of sky burials and their edification in structures like the *dakhma* or spaces like the charnel grounds. There is an irony in this, as the poem also hastened a flattening of death and its subsequent edification in the rural cemetery movement. If you've been to any municipal cemetery built during the 19th century in the United States, you've seen its effects: rolling hills and dells cloaked in arboreal splendor, lined with monuments both humble and ornate and traversed by serpentine paths. These features make for an idyllic and placid deathscape, both physically and emotionally.

The Civil War, with its meeting of archaic tactics with modern armaments, thoroughly obliterated whatever Romantic notions of death Americans still clung to. For those directly involved in the conflict, death's too-realness was readily apparent; for those insulated from the killing fields, however, the shock of witnessing their carnal truth had yet to set in. This particular trauma and its accompanying shift in thought is well exemplified by the public debut of Matthew Brady's 1862 exhibition,

"The Dead of Antietam." The exhibits, which featured photographs taken by Brady's then-employee Alexander Gardner and his assistant James Gibson, provided many with their first glimpse of the field's most bountiful crop on that mid-September day. For those who had already borne witness, it was like taking in the aftermath anew. The photographs themselves frankly revealed the frozen agony of the dead soldiers, uniformly maimed yet individually distinguishable. The multiple layers of censorship that surfaced in the wake of the exhibit's debut are also telling: woodblock reproductions of the photographs softened the soldiers' features, so that they could have collapsed just as readily from exhaustion as from a hail of minié balls. In so doing, mutilated and identifying features alike were obscured.

We seem to need that softening, for the shock of death's reality is often too bright to look at directly. In her book *When Things Fall Apart*, Pema Chödrön calls on three methods of reaching through the glare of mortal awareness toward joy: "no more struggle," "using poison as medicine," and "seeing whatever arises as enlightened wisdom." Some Tibetans maintain that the vultures congregating at charnel grounds are bodhisattvas in disguise; their effortless enactment of these methods lends credence to this belief.

Regarding the first method: vultures tend to be inactive until late morning to midday when the sun has been out long enough to thoroughly warm the earth's surface. When they finally do take flight, they take advantage of the heated air columns emanating from the sun-soaked ground. Rather than wasting energy flapping their broad wings to lift their cumbersome bodies, they allow themselves to be borne aloft on the thermals.

Regarding the second method: a buzzard's guts are a miraculous thing. There are very few obligate scavengers in nature, a key reason being that the longer a corpse decomposes, the more toxic compounds it produces. The Zoroastrians were remarkably astute in noting that a corpse will pollute the elements around it. By most biologists' accounts, however, it is not the dreaded Nasu assuming the form of a fly that contaminates the body, but rather the dead organism's own microbiota initiating the process of decomposition by dissolving it from the inside out. Vultures not only have one of the most acidic stomachs in the animal kingdom, but their intestinal microbiota also consists largely of *Clostridia* and *Fusobacteria*—bacteria found in carrion that would be lethally pathogenic in any other animal. It would seem that vultures have recruited these bacteria as

accomplices in a remarkable symbiotic feat, contributing to their ability to consume putrid meat without being poisoned by it.

Regarding the third method: what else is seeing whatever arises as enlightened wisdom, if not a different form of scavenging? In this, all the world is worshipful. I keep coming back to a time when I drove past a cow field in which several vultures were at rest, their wings outstretched and facing the setting sun. Oh, how the low-angle light caught their wing stars! Assume a horaltic pose and you cannot help but evoke a call to prayer.

I have a friend who lives with his partner in an old farmhouse. Soon after they moved in, they discovered that black vultures had nested in the barn. They don't use the space presently and have allowed the vultures to remain in residence with their nestlings. One evening during a visit, my friend took me out to the barn to introduce me. Lying at the doorstep were shreds of raccoon or possum skin, fragments of leg bone and teeth—a charnel ground not of the Tibetan plateau but the rurnt tobaccolands of the Carolina Piedmont. No sooner than we crossed the doorstep and entered the barn, there came an explosion of wings, the scraping of talons on floorboards, loud thumps in the loft. The smell was pungent, the corners of the barn a drift of feathers, bones, and splattered droppings. He motioned toward the place where their greenish eggs had lain, a patch of leftover hay in one of the mule stalls.

There was something eerily familiar in that hybrid, transitional space, where the relics of past human life had become a nesting ground. The vultures still live there, sun themselves on the porch with my friends' cats, and stay perched on the railing when they pull into the driveway. They have found a niche in my friends' lives. And mine, too, for I've found in them a lesson for how to live not only with the non-human but also with the nearness of that which scares us most.

I've been dancing around the subject so far, so let me say it straight: we're two steps away from being carrion. Worm food. Buzzards' buffet. Our individuality dissolves in death; memory is but an impression. Even monuments weather.

So? Bryant said it best: live.

Chris Robey (he/him) holds an MLA from the University of Georgia and currently works as a cultural landscape specialist with the Southeast Regional Office of the National Park Service. His poems and essays have appeared in *The Fourth River, The Peel Literature & Arts Review*, and *Permafrost Magazine*. He lives in Alexandria, Virginia with his fiber artist/librarian wife, their apple-headed tuxedo cat, and a budding collection of native perennials.

The Promise of Words

ESSAY BY EDITOR, THOMAS LLOYD QUALLS

I have written a fair amount about words. About their weight, their shyness, their resistance to being herded, their promiscuity, their demanding nature, their mystery, their alchemy, and even their quantum nature. With their remarkable abilities to teach, to communicate, to inspire, to liberate, and to seduce, they are literally the stuff of legends.

But perhaps we take it too far sometimes. We expect too much of them. We expect the words to do all the work. We expect that if we just lay them out in straight lines or in interesting patterns, they can just take it from there. But that isn't always true. We must also have willing recipients. And while words can build bridges between us, we must still walk out onto those bridges to meet each other.

Words can also be tricksters and masters of illusion. They can create their own realities and make you believe in them. That's why novels are so powerful. A writer can make up characters, a setting, and a story, and we will believe it. We will get lost in their story so much that we become attached to the characters and emotional about their fate in their make-believe world. Turns out, words in real life are no different. They are the building blocks of the stories we tell ourselves about ourselves and our world. Like novels, those stories are not necessarily true.

The music producer turned creativity guru Rick Rubin says we don't know anything. And really, doesn't that ring true? We tell ourselves so many stories our whole lives. Stories that may or may not be true. Stories that allow us to get up and put on our shoes and function in an utterly dysfunctional world. And stories that blind us to the magic that exists all around us. I wrote a whole novel about the illusions of human life. About trying to figure out what is real and what isn't. And how to believe in magic in the middle of all this sifting.

I recently wrote an essay about how one of my own stories had blinded me to an aspect of myself. About how that blindness had hurt someone who is so important to me that they are sewn into the fabric of who I am. Our stories are how that happens. We don't know something. And nature abhors a vacuum. So we decide to make up a story to fill that space. And then we live that story as if it were true. When we have no actual idea what the truth is. We are just so uncomfortable with not knowing that we'd rather make up a bad story than to sit in stillness until we can find out the truth.

I don't usually pretend to have answers to these questions that life hands to us. I just want to get better at articulating them. And at laying out some possible roadmaps. But it does seem like we need to stop writing stories we don't want to live. Because that is what happens. As soon as we write a story about our life, that is the story we live. Until we erase it. Or rewrite it.

Maybe we would do well to return to Rilke over and over, and to remember to keep asking questions. To learn to sift through the questions until we find the right ones, like puzzle pieces. And then to live those questions, instead of living our made-up answers. Instead of living the stories we throw together in an instant, to fill the void that the question leaves. Because questions leave space. They save places for answers to feel safe enough to come join us. And they also leave space for the others in our lives to come sit with us. And to solve the riddles together.

words: study 5

we do not create words,

we discover them.

words have their own identities,

their own minds, their own sense of purpose.

right and wrong, left and right, true north.

we build fences to contain them,

they slip through the rails.

we lock them in their rooms,

they move through walls.

they hide under beds, smoke cigarettes in bathrooms.

they eat junk food, read dirty magazines.

fornicate with other words.

we call words to the table.

but they may not answer or they may not eat.

words play with their food.

if you kill their spirit, they die.

lying flat on the page, translucent.

the dna of words cannot be mapped.

there's only a probability of words.

words fold space. bend time. outrun light.

Thomas Lloyd Qualls (he/him) is a writer, a condition that is apparently incurable. He is the award-winning author of two novels, and a collection of essays. He is the recipient of the Landmark Prize for Fiction and both Silver and Gold Nautilus Awards. With all his creative work, he seeks to bridge the worlds of the literary and the spiritual and to create worlds where labels are difficult to affix. Thomas lives in the high desert beauty of Northern Nevada. thomaslloydqualls.substack.com. / From the novel *Waking Up at Rembrandt's*, whose re-release from Wayfarer Books is coming in early 2026.

SEASONAL AFFECTIVE DISORDER

WILL FALK

Winter is not a woman to be overcome.
Her frigid attention is more
than a hardship to be endured.

Her cold embrace
is not meant to be escaped
for a series of tropical
one night stands with grave robbers
exhuming fossilized forests,
cremating the fallen,
combusting ancient ghosts,
and feeding the mechanical dragons
that shrink the earth with black magic
to deliver more invaders
than wooden ships ever did.

Winter does not forgive
those who lust so blindly
for her death
or "the return of light"
that they have conquered darkness
by enslaving energy,
and forcing electricity to jump
at the flick of a switch.

Winter wishes there was more time
to hide under blankets,
and to ponder cozy fires
without facing the heat.

Frostbite and hypothermia
are seasonal disorders
that Winter understands
but the gaunt, muddy corpses
of once-white polar bears prove
that you cannot hibernate
your way out of starvation.
Room temperature
simply is not a season.

And, the worst form
of seasonal affective disorder
are the delusions of those
who fuel the belief that we deserve
the comforts of warmth
and access to the labor of light
without end.

Will Falk (he/him) is a biophilic activist, author, and attorney. The natural world speaks and poetry is how Will listens. His law practice is devoted to helping Native American communities protect their sacred sites and cultural resources. He is the author of *How Dams Fall* (Homebound Publications, 2019) and *When I Set the Sweetgrass Down* (Wayfarer Books, 2023). You can follow his work at willfalk.org.

[Right] Originally from Minneapolis, **Michael Curran-Dorsand (he/him)** is an international artist, whose career as an actor, writer, and teacher has spanned the globe. He's also a proud graduate of Juilliard's Drama Division and NUI Galway's MA in Writing. His debut poetry collection *Where The Dead Poets Sing* will be released in Feb, 2026. On the stage and on the page, he draws from classical and contemporary influences, as well as a deep love of myth and storytelling in the bardic tradition.

THE INVISIBLE HAND

MICHAEL CURRAN-DORSANO

our violent delights

unhinged

with each pendulum swing,

the stalwart bolt rattling,

tarnished gold corroding

the cantilever holding

the frenzied tick-tock-tick,

the errant flick

of some invisible hand,

shadows lick the walls stretching

tall then fall, crashing

to a skittering crawl,

only to leap up to the stalls,

mercy's minister long departed there,

only empty pews scrawled

with tooth and claw,

the babel of the rabble long left to rot,

a shot rings like bell in a well,

thunderous bellowing swells,

bolt, nut and washer break,

time flies with its armament,

the shake of rafters as certain stone shatters,

what breeds in the shadows

when they lose their master?

the shots fire faster,

blood runs from the sun tipped alabaster,

no words to speak when time and mercy sleep,

deep sunk beneath the Church

of this American Dream.

NOTHING

MICHAEL CURRAN-DORSANO

for Motaz Azaiza

In a perpetual autumn,

I mourn each inky dirge droning through the headlines,

another child, another family,

another village murdered in Palestine,

their memory lives on in him,

torn limb from limb,

strewn from splintered trees

and hills of rubble, the unimaginable

absence of everything, everyone,

gone

in an instant,

screams before me beneath his

calm, collected words

the blasted heart of a man

left to wander strange shores,

to show, unflinching, what his eyes dared see,

what his camera could capture

in grace, in graves,

in gratitude, in grotesque gallantry,

living the unlivable,

the nightmare of nightmares,

and on his dark steed he rides now,

through bourgeois cafes,

well-groomed streets,

and shining capitals

to give dead eyes

their only chance to stare back.

PRECIOUS FEATHER

JOSE OSEGUERA

Nopiltze, nocuzque, noquetzale (Sweet son, my jewel, my precious feather)
—Aztec berceuse from *Daily Life of the Aztecs* by Jacques Soustelle

I brushed my thumb on his lips—across
 a sharp edge; his yawn of amniotic fluid cut
through the sterile room. Before the nurse
instructed me to grab a syringe, I lurked
near the bed like a cup of melting
ice chips. Our ferocious riptide
nursed, frustrated at mother's chest.

When I rubbed the roof of his mouth, my son
began to suckle; my pinky finger
was six strings woven from his
infinite past to my arteries.

Every swig was a tun-da-ta
tun-da-ta honing my blood;
the warmth of his sup, a secret
bolero in Agustín Lara.

His stomach, the size of a marble, craved
nectar as volcanic magma veins do freedom.
The prickle swarming my forearm—
the agony of repetitive strain or a fiery letdown—
consumed each drop inside.

"Look at him," said the nurse, "all nervous."
Her words, their sting was nothing,
the syringe, not plastic, but an extension of me:

it was my breast, my back, my strength.

His stomach emptied by the minute as mother's fountain
brimmed to shear hunger.

So I cleaved the guise of hatchet to reshape
the world with milk; I was animal,
broken surrendering to wild.

Jose Oseguera (he/him) is an LA-based writer of poetry, short fiction and literary nonfiction. His writing has been featured or is forthcoming in *Water Stone, Pinch* and *Sonora Review*. He is the author of the poetry collections *The Milk of Your Blood* (Kelsay Books, 2021) and *And This House Is Only a Nest* (Homebound Publications, 2024).

BY OUR SIDE

ROBERT BRODER

You were
JUMPING!
JUMPING!
JUMPING!
when I first saw you.
as if you were saying,
"TAKE!
ME!
HOME!"
so I did,
and named you Alice,
from the Tom Waits song.
When we left the humane society
we stopped off at a park
unhooked the leash,
you looked at me,
"I'm with you."
From that day on
you have been by our side.
You came to our wedding
on camping trips,
swimming lakes and oceans
and hiking mountains.
You adored your flying squirrel,
green blanket,
and the sunny spot in the yard.
And there was no other nighttime sleeping spot
then our bed.
You were finicky around food,
sometimes circling the bowl for hours
too nervous to eat.

A picture of you was in Stella's hospital crib
hoping she would get better.
And when the sky collapsed
and the rain pummeled,
you were by our side.
When we brought Eleanor home
you stared with uncertainty, "What is that?!"
not knowing you two would become the best of friends.
And when we rescued
two gray cats,
George and Martha, (from the picture books)
they immediately liked you
and you eventually liked them.
For over sixteen years
you were our little scrappy mutt
part chihuahua part pit bull
that was loyal and snuggly
anxious and whiney
always by our side.
We know you loved us,
and we undoubtedly
loved you.
"The skates on the pond,
they spell Alice." - Tom Waits

Robert Broder (he/him) is a picture book author, poet, and developmental editor. He likes snowy days, hiking, dogs, and coffee—preferably all four at once. Robert lives with his family in a small town, near a big lake, surrounded by green mountains. RobertBroder.com

SKY BURIAL

CONNOR WOLFE

I saw the buck laid out like a busted myth—
legs folded, belly soft, ribs skyward
like someone gave up mid-prayer.

Magpie standing proud
on the chest,
all slick tail and side-eye,
scouting the seam
between meat and morning.

First day—
fur not yet slipped,
no blood, just the hush
before the work begins.

Second day—
a hole.
　　　Third—
　　　deeper.
　　　　　　Fourth—
　　　　　　bone.

That bird knew what it was doing.
Like it had done this a hundred times—
like it had a schedule,
a union card,
a holy assignment.

By the fifth day,
it looked like a heart
still beating
in a hollow cathedral of ribs.

It didn't mourn.
Didn't flinch.
Just kept carving
its wild devotion—
answering
whatever the gods ask
a creature to do
with a body,
a hunger,
and a day.

TRUE NORTH

CONNOR WOLFE

—Along the Airline Trail, Connecticut

My deepest regrets
belong to you—
　　suspended like stars,
　　　　too distant to touch,
　　　　　　once so close
　　　　　　I could hold them.

CONNOR WOLFE (THEY/THEM) is a writer, publisher, and advocate with two decades and fourteen titles. As founder of the trans-owned Wayfarer Books and *Wayfarer Magazine*, Wolfe has earned six Pushcart Prize nominations, the Nautilus Gold Medal (2015) and Silver Medal (2022), and several *Foreword Reviews* awards. A two-term IBPA board member, Harvard graduate, and TEDx Yale speaker, they write about mental health, erasure, and the confluence of the inner and outer landscapes. In 2024, they volunteered at the Museum of Anthropology at Ghost Ranch, assisting with NAGPRA repatriation. After wintering off-grid near Cerro Pedernal, they're traveling through the San Juan Mountains—writing, creating, and wandering with their three-legged black cat, *momo*.

THE WILDEST KIND OF LOVE

HEIDI BARR

Maybe you're lost
far from home
unsure if home even exists
afraid that home is no longer there.

Many are disoriented.
Routes are long and hard.
Uncertainty abounds.
What felt stable and safe can vanish

in a blink of an eye
as a stiff wind gusts from the west
in a year that is already
beating you down.

Sorrow and fear are real
in a year like this.
Anxiety and anger are real
in a year like this.

It's normal to long to return
to what feels like home
especially when what you knew as home
might not be where you left it.

It's not easy to remember home
is with you always—a wildness
etched in your bones,
coursing through your veins,

an ancient agreement of shadow and light
a raw embodiment of love
capable of weathering
any firestorm.

But it is.
Even in a year like this.

HEIDI BARR (SHE/HER) is a writer and wellness coach whose work is founded on a commitment to cultivating ways of being that are life-giving and sustainable for people, communities, and the planet. Author of nine books and editor of two anthologies, she lives with her family on Dakota land in rural Minnesota. The above poem is included in her second poetry collection, *Slouching Toward Radiance*.

WHEN ASKED TO EXPLAIN RACISM AS A SYSTEM OF POWER, AGAIN

MATTHEW E. HENRY

after a pause, I posed a hypothetical to the class.

if all Blacks pooled
their political power
to reimpose chattel slavery
with white backs bearing the lash,
could the bill pass?

after questioning the amendments
to be repealed or replaced, wondering
which racial groups would throw in—
whites willing to wager their skin
in solidarity—they all said, no. except
the boy who misheard the question.
thought Blacks were suggesting
our own re-enslavement.

the class laughed.

but teachable moments are meant to be chased
like the North Star or a runaway slave.

the new question:
a bill to place us back in chains.
working textile factories
instead of cotton fields—
t-shirts over tobacco.
fearing assault rifles
more than whips.
with a veto-proof majority,
was it possible, even if
a Black president
sat behind the Resolute Desk?

I wish I was surprised by the silence
following their debate-less acceptance
or how it shook their white faces red.

"WON'T YOU COME AND CELEBRATE WITH ME"

MATTHEW E. HENRY

a birthday poem after Lucille Clifton

celebrate the life I've more than cobbled
overcoming the statistics and their expectations.
not dead or in prison. no hypertension or heart disease,
though I've never professionally dribbled or ran a ball.
come celebrate that I've been clean and sober
for all of my 45 years, though born in Babylon—
not white or wealthy. though bussed from red-lined land
to the high roosts of white flight, the suburbs
where I learned how to spell and correctly pronounce
"foie gras," "renaissance," and "nigger." come
celebrate my mother—a right woman of God—
to whom my father returned from buying milk
every night. celebrate them, my models for raising
the thousand kids who have skipped and shuffled
and staggered in and out of my classrooms. celebrate
my one hand holding tight to theirs, the other to necks
and frets and brass and keys and pens and pages
and the bridges between clay and starshine—both safe
and sinister. celebrate the village that raised me to know
how often my skin would warrant a clutched purse,
a shopkeeper's pursuit, a traffic stop with a glock
pointed at the back of my nappy head. come celebrate
that everyday something has tried to kill me
and has failed.

Matthew E. Henry (he/him) is an educator, essayist, and the author of six poetry collections. He is editor-in-chief of *The Weight Journal,* the creative nonfiction editor at *Porcupine Literary,* and an associate editor at *Rise Up Review.* Henry's publications include *Massachusetts Review, Ploughshares, Terrain,* and others. Matthew E. Henry earned an MFA yet continued to spend money he didn't have completing an MA in theology and a PhD in education. He writes about education, race, religion, and burning oppressive systems to the ground at www.MEHPoeting.com.

A SIGNING WITH ESTHER!

KASHAWN TAYLOR

The flyer shouts
as the barista asks what cologne I'm wearing.
The scent wafts up memories
of her father, but Voyage is cheap
& I am frugal.
The barista hands me my cookie,
blends and pours my drink,
the one with the Italian name
I cannot, at this point, remember.
My name is not asked, not written on plastic.
We are alone, until she returns from break,
asks if I have been helped. I say yes,
look at the poster to the right of her,
double take, realize she is Esther, subdued
& apron-clad, and working humbly
to support our shared dream of a writer's life.
I don't yet know what that looks like,
but Esther stays with me, in my pocket,
all day. A memento of togetherness,
       a beacon of favor.

YOU'LL FIND LOVE SOMEDAY

KASHAWN TAYLOR

Please, don't threaten me
with your fantasies of romance,
because love found me,
in these little freedoms, in words
delivered from me to you in ink & tears
& yes, in my friends, who are all my boyfriends.
Love lived in my black past, survived
my F5 winds and lightning strike venom.
If I look hard enough, hand to my face
blocking the sun, I see it still:
so much of that good shit,
blazing pink and crimson on the horizon.

Kashawn Taylor (he/him) holds a BA in English and Psychology and an MA in English and Creative Writing. Before his incarceration, he built a strong academic foundation, which he continues to develop in prison. His writing has appeared in publications such as *POETRY, Prison Journalism Project, The Blotter Magazine, Minutes Before Six, Evening Street Review's DIY Prison Project,* and *Indiana Review.*

SMOKE GHOST OF THE OLIVE TREES TALKS BACK

EMILIE LYGREN

"Israeli Settlers have deliberately burned or cut down
hundreds of olive trees in the West Bank." —the UN

We had a thousand more seeds hidden in our arms
one for every year of our combined lives.

Could you not tolerate that much abundance?
Were you threatened by how easefully
we swallow sun and bear fruit,
find the hands of our careful people
and travel with them through all of their days,
all of their seasons, all of their meals—

all of,
olive,
prayer.

Where do you get your cooking oil?
How far does it travel to reach you?
How loud will you lie about where it came from?

Our steady green leaves are a song
written with desert air.

Now our bodies will join the clouds.
May our truth rain incessantly.
May we flood you with the echo of what you've done.

Emilie Lygren (she/her) is a poet, educator, and naturalist whose work is grounded in curiosity and reverence. She is a professor of creative writing, a poet in the schools, and author of the book, *What We Were Born For.* Find more of her work and words at emilielygren.com.

IN THE BEGINNING,
THERE WAS DARKNESS—

REBECCA BRENNER

I looked for you there.
Feet fire in the reservoir
pushing the smallest of waves

I wanted you, then

to settle and rest beside me.
But you're always so worried—
pacing the shore.

Even the dog, panting,

catches every stick tossed
now crane wings spread
breath rises over the sun.

I began—

milk and milkway.
in the upper regions of sky
art was always a body

poetry an ear
music, bone.
I loved her deeply—

when language owned fire.

So why am I here?
Interrupt the pattern—

Beasts and plants were never bound
never wired for this oppression

NAME THE WILDFLOWERS, GATHER
THEM GENTLY FOR HER:

REBECCA BRENNER

Stickseeds sing violet—
know each other by touch,

Sulphur cinquefoil, pale yellow, delicate
find one another in an embrace

Sticky geranium—what are you, fuchsia? Checkerblooms?
Molecules bond, electrons share,

Chicory, sun-washed in purple and green
how strange we were taught the universe is sterile,

Showy goldeneye, like miniature sunflowers
certainly nothing exists in isolation

Pass by the paintbrushes—too explosive to pick
the imagined secular vessel broken

Common yarrow, Prairie sunflowers—soon taller than me
a terrible lie, this separation—

Leave the glacier lily—too soft to hold
ordered within narrow rules, s sky, is wind, is rain.

Rebecca Brenner (she/her) is a writer, journalist, and mindfulness meditation teacher. Her work has appeared in *TIME*, the *Los Angeles Times, Tin House*, and elsewhere. She serves as president and co-founder of Mindful. Summit County, a nonprofit devoted to mindfulness as a tool for community care, and is active in local LGBTQ+ advocacy and community-building efforts. *Paper House* is her debut memoir-in-verse—a personal reckoning with the intergenerational impact of addiction, loss, and the enduring bonds that continue.

LIVING AMONG CANNIBALS

LANCE LE GRYS

the proportion of cannibals now living among us
as demonstrated in the most recent census
has surpassed fifty percent
that is to say
cannibals are no longer living among us
we are living among them

I considered joining one of the demonstrations
against cannibalism
to take a stand
make my voice heard
not against cannibals against cannibalism
hate the sin love the sinner

but then I was made aware
of well documented reports from several prominent
research institutes
demonstrating
the almost complete integration of cannibalism
in the greater economy
a demonstration difficult to ignore
you can't buy a stick of gum or a car battery without
at some stage along the supply chain
ingesting
at least implicitly
some small cut of human flesh
diluted in a weak broth

turnout in any case was pitifully small
and largely made up of people of a sort one
would not wish to be identified with

instead I went to a cafe
to order the special
liver of an alcoholic
having always had a weakness
for pickled meats

Mica L. Rich (they/them) is a New England poet whose work explores trauma, healing, and identity through vulnerability. Their debut collection, *This Is How Wildflowers Grow*, is available through Barnes & Noble, and their poetry appears in journals such as *The Avocet* and *Inkwell*. Mica organizes with Slam Free or Die, edits for the *Poetry Society of New Hampshire*, and teaches, tutors, and edits freelance.

Lance Le Grys (he/him) is the author of the poetry collection *Views from an Outbuilding* (Clare Songbirds Publishing House, 2019) and the chapbook *Pilate Suite* (Bottlecap Press).. His work has appeared in many publications, including *America, Caveat Lector, The Naugatuck River Review, The Lullwater Review, The West Trade Review, Knock*, and *The Southern Humanities Review*. A selection of his songwriting indiscretions can be heard at legrys.bandcamp.com. His web site is at lancelegrys. wordpress.com. He lives in Castleton, Vermont

M/F/X

MICA L. RICH

When I cough up the word
"woman"
It doesn't come up willing,
drags
through my throat like sandpaper,
resistance at every inch,
getting caught in the layers
of lace and white lies when
I spit it out.

Like how I used to
trace the glee
down the curves of my silhouette,
revel in the excitement
of a little black dress until
I caught the hunger
in someone else's gaze,
corset tight, reminding me
these clothes were never
made for my enjoyment,
are only
the pretty place setting
for a meal some man's been waiting
to sink their teeth into.
No matter how I change
the package I can't
convince them I am anything
but consumable,
Can't even convince myself
I'll outlive this expiration date.
How quickly I learned
to be confined
by someone else's expectations.
Stepped forward to fill
the hollow outline of a woman,
did what was demanded believing I needed
the praise to prove I was real.
How ironic, I forgot my own
fluid truth in the process.

Sometimes,
(when I'm high)
I realize how much time
I spend avoiding my own face
in the mirror, so detached
its like dressing a doll,
and I, the ghost inside,
am all too aware
how no part of me is still
mine
from the moment I'm perceived.

I cling to "nonbinary"
like the last life raft, but how
can I be sure
if I know who I am,
or if all I know
is that being a woman
just feels too unsafe.

Sometimes
I want the freedom
to look like a woman.
But not 'woman' in the way
it rolls lazily off the tongue.
Less 'woman'
as Eve was to Adam
and more
Immortal Fae Creature,
Unknowable Cosmic Entity
artfully disguised inside
the shape of a woman.

The kind of woman who,
when I wear a suit, you
do a double take, unsure what looked
so feminine in the first place,
while I
hold up the glamor
of a gentle masculinity
in the way I weigh
my hands down with metal,
draw the eye

to less delicate lines like
I can convince you this jawline
is more chiseled
just by willing it to be.

I'll keep fighting to find
the best fit for my features,
and every time lose the battle
over this body when
I never wanted it
to begin with.

I want to be soul,
and smoke,
and stardust,

I want to be
all Florence
and even more Machine

all Mad Hatter,
endless tea party
the ambiguity
between genius and insanity
I want to be ageless
timeless,

always in motion,
to hold an ancient secret
in the upturned corner
of my lips, so enticing you
have to lean in to hear it.

If I am going
to be seen as a woman
all I want
is for the choice
to be mine.

DEAREST MEFITIS,

Squuncke   Tiskáy   Maká   Mephitis mephitis*

GWENDOLYN MORGAN

Every evening at sunset we are grateful for your presence
the goddess of liminal spaces and trance inducing vapors
you walk past us foraging for hazelnuts, blackberries, insects
pause, look at us cautiously wait for the ICE vehicle to pass
as we drink peppermint tea in filbert-brown pottery mugs.

*

Mama skunk, you blink, turn your head, offer a kinglet-like chirp
little squunckes scamper up the earthen steps, follow you
past Sword and Bracken Fern, Crab Apple, and Cherry Tree,
slipping out of sight into the Atfalati Kalapuya Camas Meadows
the riparian woodlands and wetlands of this place.

*

Nocturnal, insectivorous yet omnivorous
determined, black pelage with a thin white stripe along their dulcet faces
white marking on their nape which runs along their spine,

Striped Skunks have a high mortality rate, due to vulnerability
loss of habitat, increased use of pesticides, animal control.
Defensive, courageous, known for an odiferous, sulfurous musk,
we have seen them stamp the ground in warning
before lifting their tail and back legs.

*

Act up, speak out, move on before it is too late
perhaps you offer us a black & white teaching in this divided time
as we metaphorically line our running shoes with skunk skin
to navigate the territory ahead.

---

*Algonquian, Kalapuya Atfalati, Lakota, Latin names for Skunk
Ancestor warriors lined their moccasins with skunk skin for protection

ANCESTRAL FLIGHT PATTERNS, PALETTES

GWENDOLYN MORGAN

Red-shafted Flicker, chevrons on her breast
red-orange shaft of feather
amongst Sword Ferns, sap green to jade green

after heat dome   burnt-red tips of Western Red Cedar
like COVID spikes, spikes of heat, anger, wildfires
foliage scorch and heat stress, community stress

loss of our ancestral compass
White-tailed deer with severe mange   decimation of our constitution
Mariupol, then innumerable bombings of hospitals in Ukraine,

Afghanistan, Gaza, Sudan, places we don't even know, violence un-nameable
hunger, famine, the sorrow of the borderlands, this county, our country
children, do not forget the children, our descendants

wires stretched taut, slab walls along the Mexican border, indigenous women missing
intentional puncture railroad spike in our truck tire, pile of human excrement left alongside

violence from neighbor, stab of sorrow, racism
homophobia, transphobia, xenophobia, malicious harassment

then, my grandmother's paintings—stretched linen canvas with a floral background
Sunflowers, Hollyhock, Gerbera Daisies, White-tailed Deer
memories of opossum, raccoon, chickaree, stoat.

We wander in a sanctuary of grief
pools of hope and gratitude like her watercolor palette
hand-filled, full pan colors, granulating shades

we return to this cathedral of cedars
where three deer gather in the center
Red-shafted Flicker, candlewick of light.

We re-turn.   We re-member.

We return.   We remember.

Gwendolyn Morgan (she/her) is a Pacific Northwest poet, hospice/animal chaplain and artist. *Flight Feathers*, her fourth book of poetry (Wayfarer Books), found its filoplumes at Centrum Artist Residency and is a Nautilus Gold Winner in lyric prose and hybrid works. She served as Clark County Poet Laureate 2018-2020. Gwendolyn and her spouse Judy infuse their poetry and music with elements from the natural world. As a queer multiracial family in a multispecies watershed, they are committed to hospitality and welcome for all.

IDENDROCHRONOLOGY OF A GUN

CLAIRE CAMPO

Play the one about the Chinese Buddhist alchemist,
about charcoal, honey, saltpeter & sulfur
The first firework, whose eyes awed to wonder,
under what moon what sky did they collide?
Skip to track 13, all flintlock and blunderbuss,
burning match lit fuse of who decided you could die like this?
Some metalsmith. In Kentucky, Ohio, or Pennsylvania.
Improved aim (hunting game)
Play the song of the First Bullet and the First Deer,
what music they make turned militia.
To the tune of a minute to load a single shot.

What sound does the armory make?
Knowing it holds only steel death,
only the fated ricochet of no home.
Track 1776. Deringer, Remington,
Eli Whitney with the moving parts,
no dance for this flint, it's 1836,
it's Colt 45 and two zig-zags.

It's how a rabbit runs, knows it is prey
zig-zags threat evasion, to tire the predator.
A rabbit can run up to 30 mph,
bullets don't get tired.
2700 miles an hour,
three times faster than an airplane.
I can't translate flying.
Don't run in a straight line.

Track 45: A double-barrel shotgun
wasn't fast enough.
The Browning automatic rifle was in style for
Bonnie and Clyde and WW2.
Track 47: Iraq, Iran, Saudi Arabia, Afghanistan,
Boston marathon, Ukraine, Gaza.
There are no small wars, no small worlds

Track 19: A school shooting isn't loud enough for anyone to hear,
how we rationalize the sound of something familiar
popped plastic bag,
backpack dropping, mental illness.
Silence doesn't do it justice.
Play the one about the NRA
go ahead, I'll wait.
Play the one about Uvalde how they waited,
to the tune of 2700 miles an hour
to the tune of Kalashnikov
did you know an AK-47 can live for 20-40 years?
Easy to relocate and reuse.
Kalashnikov, a slave of god, of gun.
He says he sleeps soundly
He's dead now too no man's god is a gun.
Play the one about the ...
Was it fireworks or a gun?
Listen for the cadence

Claire Campo (she/her) is a poet, actor, and teaching artist whose work pushes boundaries in form and language. Co-founder of Poetic Justice, a literacy and poetry program for carceral settings, Claire's surreal, experimental style explores identity and cultural memory. Their short film, *i love you like science,* received the Linklater Award for Best Dialogue at the Austin Arthouse Film Festival, and their poetry has appeared in *This Land Press, Emerge Magazine, New Words Press, and Super Present Magazine.* Of Mohawk, French, and Dutch descent, Claire is dedicated to revitalizing Indigenous narratives as a member of the Six Nations of the Grand River.

"WE'RE ALL BORN NAKED AND THE REST IS DRAG"

CHRIS WATKINS

Look me in the eye and call me a fag,
this skirt will still look good on me.
We're all born naked and the rest is drag.

Laugh at my makeup. Point out my bag.
Tell me I'm only good on my knees.
Look me in the eye and call me a fag.

This body was born with the art of the brag:
I'm the prettiest, handsomest, glamorous she.
We're all born naked. The rest is a drag

if you shop in one section, live like a tag
on your least favorite shirt. Spill the real tea:
look yourself in the eye when you call me a fag.

Baby, I'm not your mother and don't mean to nag,
but deep in your pockets, don't you agree
that we're all born naked and the rest is drag?

Then pull up your panties. Pin up your wig.
Put on a skirt and come follow me.
I'll look in your eyes, fly you a new flag
cause we're all born naked, and the rest is drag.

SONNET FROM THE CLOSET

CHRIS WATKINS

There's a tinted revolving door in here.
Every time I come out, I'm still in the closet.
Saw a therapist for all my Lutheran fears—
doused hell's candle, now it's dark in the closet.
Out shopping in heels and lipstick and lace,
got a whole new wardrobe still in the closet.
Watched Nancy Pelosi come on Drag Race
and say get to the poles (or get back in the closet).
I travel, am tolerable in most states' cities.
Like the tabernacle, I carry the closet.
The kind of white person white liberals pity.
It's easy to think of yourself in the closet.
Praise Marsha P. Johnson's first brick at the riot,
but we're still in the stone walls of the closet.

Chris Watkins they/them is a genderqueer poet, writer, and environmental activist living in Tallahassee, FL. They earned their PhD in poetry and ecocriticism at Florida State University and currently serve as the Academics and Partnerships Coordinator of FSU's Sustainable Campus. Chris's recent work has appeared in *Poetry Magazine*, *Cincinnati Review*, and *The Harvard Review* among other journals. Their debut collection, *The Drag Gospel of Queer Jesus,* is forthcoming with Saturnalia Books.

FORESTER

JEFFERY BERG

Even if fleeting, to be someone
who treks the weedy hill as a nobody.
Tree on the far field, a revelation.

Secretly, I watch him on the mountain.
I talk the voice of him I embody,
even if fleeting, to be someone.

Unsure, in search of, here I was hidden
in cracked green glass, old commodity.
Tree on the far field, a revelation,

and then sawed through. I saw through the woodsman
his hands rough and sapped to work my body.
Even if fleeting, to be someone

out in the dew-damp wilds, a creation.
I jack, I slack, I clasp androgyny.
Tree on the far field, a revelation.

It speaks wood, it speaks a voice to summon
the match flung to burn old property.
Even if fleeting, to be someone's
tree on a far field, a revelation.

[Right] Born and raised in Los Angeles, **Michael Roque (they/them)** discovered his love for poetry and prose amid friends on the bleachers of Pasadena City College. Now he currently lives in the Middle East and is being inspired by the world around him. His poems have been published by literary magazines like *North Dakota Quarterly, Cholla Needles, The Literary Hatchet* and others.

Jeffery Berg's (he/they) poems have appeared in various journals such as *Pine Hills Review* and most recently, *Same Faces Collective*. Jeffery lives between Jersey City and Provincetown and reviews films for Film-Forward. His debut poetry collection, *Re-Animator*, is forthcoming from Indolent Books in 2026.

AN EMERGENCY ROOM WE CALL A NATION

MICHAEL ROQUE

A year of in-betweens
in a vibrant life
now resembling an ER waiting room—
people-packed in varying states of anguish.
Those wheelchair-bound, abandoned in halls,
those bedridden, speaking in groans
and the many—
sitting, standing seemingly unfazed,
but to an extent all commonly feeling pain,
a need for a doctor we don't see,
a need for the aches to be eased,
but malnourished on stretchers—
Our only medics.

Beeps, screams.
Whines, cries.
Rushing feet,
panicked eyes
and another flatline
to collectively ring in every ear.

Heave—
heave—
heave—
Wait— and breathe,
wait— and breathe.
I squeeze the sweat-soaked sheets,
as my soul strains through me by the second,
deflating my being like a liferaft with a leak,
leaving me stagnant in a drowning situation
calling for patience.
Patience, while feeling a cast iron rod
pierce through my heart,
clog my throat,

prod my brain.
Patience, while plowing through another day
by the grace of a caffeine-powered body.
By the mercy of a mind hoping tomorrow
might rebirth a fallen yesteryear
to remind me—
I'm of worth.

At last, doctor calls my name,
fires questions out the mouth like a Mossberg 500
and rushes away for another four months,
leaving more holes in a leaking plot needing to be filled.
No surgery nor novocaine
just more stagnance in a room
where spinning ceiling fans are the only movement seen—
the sole motion
spreading around everyone's disease.

Am I far off somewhere?
Daydreaming in a car stuck in a roundabout,
having a bad trip in a brighter year,
or am I really trapped in an unending day?
An ER kept alive by insomnia
and a newly discovered inability
to walk through chaotic hallways—
'cause never failing to freeze
are two legs
locking me
between entrance and exit—
stranding me
in a smothering embrace.

(TO WHAT WE BEAR WITNESS IS OUR STORY TO TELL)

RICK BENJAMIN

in memory of Daunte Wright

She is just out of Greek
tragedy central casting

& he, he's stuck in a role
she thinks she's already

seen him play: black man
stopped by police which's

also to say, her, woman
among men for twenty-6

some odd years made to
do scut-work; she's never

even fired her gun, tazer,
always gets stuck with a

new trainee still trying to
show she's just as good a

cop as any man, when she
maybe sees an expired tag,

not illegal, but also an air-
freshener hanging from a

rearview, which is. His re-
cords clean she's shocked

to see: after all he's a black
man, but she's got the lead

(she's with the trainee) &,
soon enough she's a white

woman in charge among a
gaggle of white men all of
them hell-bent on getting
him out of his car because
of an air freshener hanging
on the rearview. How he's

used that same mirror, dbl-
consciousness, watching all

assemble round his car. He
already knows that he can't

take this injustice too far,
but he sure as hell isn't

getting out of this car
seeing as containment

of terror's the only play
he's got,

Ma'am? so much courtesy
in the middle of rough &

rude, he can tell she's no
good, too, just another one

of the guys, & also, already,
there'll be no wise or reason

for what
comes next:

another black man
driving,

while dead.

(AMERICA NEVER WAS AMERICA TO ME),

RICK BENJAMIN

after Langston Hughes

but it was to you?
& him, too? Who

am I to say what
was, wasn't, or,

for that matter
what is or isn't

true? I will say
nothing's new,

that freedom's
just for a chosen

few, also that it
won't do, this

promise long
past due, & so

many singing
the blues, bop,

Bach & Bessie
too. You, me,

then America
will be.

DRILL

RICK BENJAMIN

The teacher said to get under our desks,
crouch down as if in prayer & place
our hands behind our necks.

It was a weekly drill: what to do
in case of sudden nuclear war. Our
teacher said we should be perfectly

still, &, also, closed the door. As I
curled my body into position on
the cold, dirty floor, I felt safer

than I did at home, where explosions
of a different kind were a daily
occurrence. Here there was talk

of deterrents, having more bombs
than someone else, how these
would prevent consequences

we wouldn't be able to defend
ourselves against. A bell rang
to signal all clear, but I knew

I was still going home that night,
no saving desk in sight.

Rick Benjamin (he/him) lives on unceded Chumash land in Goleta, California, and walks each day on indigenous trails. He teaches courses at the University of California Santa Barbara, among them poetry and community, the wild literature of ecology, and literatures of both social and juvenile justice, while also working among elders, young people at a local Boys and Girls Club, in art museums and youth detention facilities. He served as the poet laureate of Rhode Island from 2012 – 2016.

IN THE COURT OF KING FRIDAY

LEE SEIGEL

The times you fight best are when backed into a corner with dirty hands and aching feet,
your teeth bared, licking blood from your lips. They swing high but you dodge artfully, a
pirouette in the alley moonlight;

made possible by viewers like you.

This is love-letter to you, Fred, as I wake up from a nap to Jacques julienning a dozen
potatoes, steel glinting under the hot TV lights, this is where we learn

our justice.

My gut says to rage and lunge for the throat of the beast
that would deprive us of Julia's heavenly Bourguignon--

but You (loving me just the way I am) would not want that, and to disappoint that face,
young in the '60s, making Congress cry, would be the most grievous of sins.

If only I could stop, but with everything on the line,
how can I pledge anything less?

There is something deep inside, clawing hot
up the back of the throat, rancid tasting, full of bile and wrath and tears,

a ruinous fury that anyone would take you away, out of spite and pettiness and for no
other reason than because they can.

Where are the helpers you promised? Because I don't want to stop, I want to fight to
save it all for you, and Julia, and Bob, with his happy little trees.

I want those monsters to hurt, the fiends who would burn your legacy to the ground
and dance in the ashes, soot-stained suits billowing in the breeze.

I cannot stop, I need to fight, and may become unlovely, though with love in my heart.

Would you still be mine?

Lee Seigel (he/him) is a fundraising, operations, and I.T. professional, who pursues his passions for travel, photography, and poetry, often all at once. He is the author of the collection, *A Season or So,* and was the Heidi Knecht Memorial Award winner at the 2022 Ohio Poetry Day Competition. Originally from Long Island, New York, he now lives in Ohio with his wife, son, and spoiled cats.

"THE UNDERGROUND FREQUENCY"

BY *WAYFARER MAGAZINE*
MIX MEDIA WITH MANIPULATION BY
ADOBE FIREFLY. © 2025.

EMERGENCY SUPPORT & CRISIS HOTLINES

Trans Lifeline—translifeline.org

U.S. (877-565-8860) | Canada (877-330-6366) Trans Lifeline remains a peer-run crisis line staffed by trans people for trans and questioning people. Their hotline is anonymous and does not engage in non-consensual active rescue. Hours are Monday–Friday 10 AM–6 PM Pacific (1 PM–9 PM Eastern). Spanish-language support is available.

LGBTQIA++ National Help Center—lgbthotline.org

888-843-4564 (general) The Help Center provides confidential peer support via several lines: the National Hotline, Coming-Out Support Line, Youth Talkline, and Senior Hotline. Hours are Monday–Friday 11 AM–8 PM Pacific (2 PM–11 PM Eastern) and Saturday 9 AM–2 PM Pacific.

The Trevor Project—thetrevorproject.org

1-866-488-7386 or text "START" to 678-678 Trevor Project continues to offer 24/7 crisis counseling for LGBTQIA+ youth via phone, chat or text. The service is free, confidential and available across the U.S..

StrongHearts Native Helpline—strongheartshelpline.org

844-762-8483 A culturally responsive helpline for Indigenous LGBTQ2S+ people experiencing domestic or sexual violence. It operates 24/7 and offers confidential support.

RAINN (National Sexual Assault Hotline)—rainn.org

800-656-4673 (HOPE) RAINN operates the national hotline for survivors of sexual violence. LGBTQIA+-inclusive support is available by phone, online chat or text.

988 Suicide & Crisis Lifeline (U.S.)—988lifeline.org

Dial 988 The 988 Lifeline provides confidential support 24/7 for anyone in emotional crisis. As of July 2025 the specialized "Press 3" option for LGBTQIA+ youth has been discontinued under the current U.S. administration; however, LGBTQIA+ callers can still receive culturally competent support by calling, texting or chatting via the general line. The lifeline's website offers tips and safety-plan resources.

LEGAL RESOURCES & KNOW-YOUR-RIGHTS

Transgender Law Center (TLC)—transgenderlawcenter.org

TLC remains a leading U.S. trans-led legal advocacy organization. Its Legal Information Helpdesk provides information about laws and policies affecting trans people. Contact: Phone 510-587-9696, collect line for incarcerated people 510-380-8229, email info@transgenderlawcenter.org.

Lambda Legal—lambdalegal.org

Provides legal assistance and strategic litigation for LGBTQIA+ and HIV-positive individuals. Regional helpdesk phone numbers include: New York (212-809-8585), Los Angeles (213-382-7600), Chicago (312-663-4413), Dallas (214-219-8585) and Washington D.C. (202-804-6245). Call your regional office to request legal help.

ACLU LGBTQIA+ Rights Project—aclu.org/issues/lgbtq-rights

The ACLU advocates for LGBTQIA+ rights nationwide. People who experience discrimination based on sexual orientation or gender identity can complete the "Report LGBTQIA+ and HIV Discrimination" intake form on the site.

Sylvia Rivera Law Project (SRLP)—srlp.org

Offers free legal services for low-income trans, non-binary and gender non-conforming people, with a focus on Black and Brown communities. The office is at 133 W 19th Street, 6th Floor, New York, NY 10011; phone 212-337-8550

GLBTQ Legal Advocates & Defenders (GLAD)—glad.org

GLAD provides legal advocacy and a confidential infoline for LGBTQIA+ New Englanders. Reach their main office at 617-426-1350 or email gladlaw@gladlaw.org. The GLAD Law Answers infoline accepts voicemails at 800-455-GLAD and emails at GLADLawAnswers@GLADLaw.org

LEGAL RESOURCES & KNOW-YOUR-RIGHTS, CONTINUED

Gender Justice—genderjustice.us

litigates gender-based cases in the U.S. Midwest and offers resources for trans people navigating discrimination. Healthcare & Medical Resources

Planned Parenthood (LGBTQIA+ Services)—plannedparenthood.org

Many Planned Parenthood health centers offer gender-affirming hormone therapy, puberty blockers, surgery referrals and transition support for trans men, trans women and non-binary people. Check with local clinics for available services.

World Professional Association for Transgender Health (WPATH) wpath.org

WPATH develops the internationally recognized Standards of Care and offers a provider directory and training for clinicians treating trans patients.

Callen-Lorde Community Health Center—callen-lorde.org (New York City)

Provides trans-inclusive primary care, hormone therapy, mental health services, STI screening and HIV prevention. Chelsea clinic (212) 271-7200, Bronx clinic (718) 215-1800, Brooklyn clinic (718) 215-1818.

Point of Pride—pointofpride.org

After merging with the Jim Collins Foundation in January 2025, Point of Pride administers the Annual Trans Surgery Fund, providing grants for gender-affirming surgeries and free binders and femme shapewear.

Local Queer-Friendly Clinics

Many community clinics have introduced specialized trans health programs since 2024. Examples include the VIP Mental Health Center and Alexis Project (Los Angeles) for Medi-Cal recipients and Bienestar (L.A. County) offering hormone care, HIV services and food bank assistance.

A QUEER & TRANS RESOURCE LIST

LEGAL RESOURCES & KNOW-YOUR-RIGHTS CONT...

MENTAL HEALTH & WELLNESS SUPPORT

Inclusive Therapists—inclusivetherapists.com

A directory of mental health professionals affirming of LGBTQIA+ and BIPOC identities. They offer a free "get-matched" service and maintain a list of crisis warm lines, emphasizing police-free support.

National Queer & Trans Therapists of Color Network (NQTTCN)

Provides a directory of culturally competent mental-health providers for queer and trans people of color. Recommended by AANHPI mental-health a rticles as a resource for QTPOC communities.

Therapy for Black Girls—therapyforblackgirls.com

Offers a therapist locator, podcast and resources aimed at Black women and non-binary people seeking culturally responsive care.

The Okra Project—theokraproject.com

Provides mutual aid and mental-health support for Black trans people. Programs include funding for therapy through a partnership with BetterHelp, a rides and meals fund, holiday groceries and rent/utility assistance.

National Queer Asian Pacific Islander Alliance (NQAPIA)—nqapia.org

Offers multilingual coming-out guides and family acceptance resources for queer and trans API families. While not a counseling provider, the site is a gateway to culturally specific support.

Thrive Lifeline—thrivelifeline.org

A peer-run crisis text line for marginalized communities (including trans and BIPOC individuals) listed on Trans Can Work's resource list.

MUTUAL AID & COMMUNITY SUPPORT

For the Gworls—forthegworls.party

A Black trans-led collective that raises funds through parties to assist with rent, gender-affirming surgery costs, medication and travel. The organization invites applications for assistance through its website.

Black Trans Advocacy Coalition (BTAC)—blacktrans.org

Provides housing, employment, basic-needs assistance and healthcare for Black trans people. Their help line operates Tuesday-Thursday 10 AM–2 PM Central, phone 855-624-7715.

Emergency Release Fund (NYC)—emergencyreleasefund.com

Offers interest-free loans to help pay bail or bond for trans, gender-nonconforming and intersex people in New York City who are detained. The fund is volunteer-run and relies on donations.

Marsha P. Johnson Institute (MPJI)—marshap.org

MPJI protects the rights of Black trans people through advocacy, organizing and a resource map that lists culturally competent services for housing, food, legal aid and wellness.

Trans Housing Coalition (Atlanta)—transhousingcoalition.org

Uses a Housing First model to secure permanent housing for chronically unhoused trans and gender-nonconforming people in Atlanta. Applicants must be trans, currently unhoused and living in Atlanta.

Mutual-Aid Microgrants—Trans Empowerment Project

TEP launched a microgrant program in 2024/25 to provide direct financial assistance to Two-Spirit, trans, intersex and gender-expansive (2TIGE) individuals. The General Assistance Fund helps cover urgent expenses such as housing, medical care, food and transportation; grant applications were open in early 2024 and awards announced in April 2024. TEP also offers advocacy groups (Inmate Advocacy Project, Trans Mentorship, etc.) via its website.

INTERNATIONAL SUPPORT & ASYLUM

ILGA World—ilga.org

A global federation of 2,000+ organizations advocating for LGBTQIA+ rights. ILGA World provides country-specific legal resources and publishes annual State of the World reports.

Transgender Europe (TGEU)—tgeu.org

A membership organization working for trans rights in Europe and Central Asia. TGEU maintains tools like the Trans Rights Index & Map, Trans Murder Monitoring and Trans Health Map.

Rainbow Railroad—rainbowrailroad.org

Assists LGBTQIA+ people facing persecution by relocating them to safer countries. The organization provides emergency travel support and works with governments to facilitate resettlement.

OutRight International—outrightinternational.org

Advocates for LGBTIQ rights globally. Offers emergency grants for activists and documents human-rights abuses. Contact: New York office (212-430-6054); general email hello@outrightinternational.org.

Astraea Lesbian Foundation for Justice—astraeafoundation.org

A public foundation funding global LGBTQIA+ activism.
Headquarters: 421 8th Ave #2752, New York, NY 10116-2752; phone +1 212 529-8021.

ORAM (Organization for Refuge, Asylum & Migration)—oramrefugee.org

ORAM advocates for LGBTIQIA+ asylum seekers and refugees worldwide. It documents abuses, trains refugee professionals and works to remove systemic barriers.

Trans Asylum Seeker Support Network (TASSN)—transasylumsupportnetwork

An interdependent network in western Massachusetts dedicated to freeing trans asylum seekers from detention and helping them build lives in the U.S. The network links asylum seekers with sponsors and mutual-aid resources, advocating abolition of detention and borders.

HOUSING & SHELTER

Trans Housing Coalition (Atlanta)

see Mutual Aid Provides permanent housing for Atlanta's unhoused
trans and gender-nonconforming people.

Ali Forney Center—aliforneycenter.org (New York City)

Offers emergency and transitional housing, drop-in services, medical care,
job readiness and mental-health counseling for LGBTQIA+ homeless youth.
New intakes are accepted Monday–Friday 8 AM–8 PM and weekends 10 AM–6 PM;
contact (212) 206-0574 ext 100.

True Colors United—truecolorsunited.org

Focuses on ending youth homelessness through advocacy, training
and technical assistance with an emphasis on LGBTQIA+ and BIPOC youth.

My Sistah's House—mshmemphis.org (Memphis, TN)

Provides emergency housing, tiny-house construction and advocacy
for Black trans women and gender-nonconforming people.
Contact (901) 352-1660; donors can support by texting MSH to 26989.

Openhouse SF—openhousesf.org (San Francisco)

Builds community and provides housing for LGBTQIA+ seniors through
affordable housing complexes and support services.

Micro Rainbow (UK)

see International Support Offers safe temporary housing for LGBTQIA+
asylum seekers; partner with Refugee Action and Rainbow Migration.

T4T Caregiving (t4tcaregiving.org)

A grassroots collective of trans caregivers and doulas offering sliding-scale care for
trans people undergoing gender-affirming surgeries anywhere in the U.S..

SAVE · SHARE · SUPPORT >>
QR CODE · FREE PRINTABLE PDF

EMPLOYMENT & JOB SUPPORT

Trans Can Work—transcanwork.org

A non-profit creating inclusive workplaces for gender-diverse people. Current programs include the State of California Career Services Program (open to California residents) and the Amity Foundation Work Re-Entry Program for formerly incarcerated TGI individuals in LA County. They also maintain a job board and a comprehensive resource spreadsheet with legal, medical and mental-health services.

TransWork (Philadelphia)—transwork.org

Connects trans job seekers with affirming employers, hosts job fairs and offers resume and interview coaching. The program encourages employers to undergo trans-inclusion training.

Transgender District (San Francisco)—transgenderdistrictsf.com

The first legally recognized transgender cultural district. Programs include name- and gender-change assistance, a social-justice fellowship, TGNC health and wellness fair, entrepreneurship accelerator and an emergency Riot Fund for trans-led organizations.

Trans Employment Project (TEP)—part of Trans Empowerment Project

Offers job-readiness support and mentorship for 2TIGE individuals.

Fortitude Fund (pridefoundation.org)

Established by the Pride Foundation in 2025 to support organizations serving trans communities facing urgent needs, particularly in regions affected by anti-trans legislation.

International Trans Fund (transfund.org)

Provides global grant funding to trans-led organizations

EDUCATION & SCHOLARSHIPS

Trans Student Educational Resources (TSER)—transstudent.org

TSER is relaunching its scholarship program. The organization noted that its national trans-specific scholarship fund intends to restart in 2025 after previous rounds in 2021–22. TSER also runs the Trans Youth Leadership Summit and provides infographics and training.

Point Foundation Scholarships—pointfoundation.org

Awards scholarships to LGBTQIA+ students with an emphasis on leadership and community involvement.

Pride Foundation (US Northwest)—pridefoundation.org

Offers scholarships for LGBTQIA+ students in Alaska, Idaho, Montana, Oregon and Washington.

Human Rights Campaign (HRC)
Scholarship Database—hrc.org/resources/scholarships

Maintains an updated database of scholarships and fellowships for LGBTQIA+ and allied students, including trans-specific awards.

Campus Pride—campuspride.org/scholarships

Provides a searchable list of LGBTQIA+ scholarships and fellowships across the U.S. It also hosts a Trans Policy Clearinghouse for college policies.

MUTUAL-AID FOR GENDER AFFIRMING CARE

GenderBands (genderbands.org)

Offers grants covering a wide range of transition costs—including surgeries, hormone therapy, electrolysis, haircuts, clothing, and name-change fees. Grants typically open in the fall.

Black Trans Men Top Surgery Grant (blacktransmen.org)

Provides up to $1,000 toward gender-affirming top surgery for Black/African-American trans men in the U.S..

TransMission (loftgaycenter.org)

Gives up to $500 for expenses tied to social, legal, medical, or surgical transition; priority goes to residents of New York's Hudson Valley but applications are open nationwide.

Campaign for Southern Equality
Trans Youth Emergency Project (southernequality.org)

Provides emergency grants and logistical support to families of trans youth needing to travel out of state for care.

North Texas TRANSportation Network

Offers travel grants for North Texas families seeking out-of-state gender-affirming health care for trans and gender-diverse minors.

South Dakota Trans Resilience Fund (transformationprojectsd.org)

Supplies mini-grants to families traveling out of state for gender-affirming care.

SECURE MESSING & CALLING APPS

Signal—signal.org

End-to-end encrypted messaging, voice, and video calls.
No ads, metadata protection, and open-source security.
Best for: Private conversations, organizing, whistleblowing.

Session—getsession.org

Anonymous, decentralized messaging app with no phone number required.
Messages are routed through multiple nodes, hiding your location.
Best for: Highly anonymous communication.

Threema—threema.ch (Paid, but highly secure)

No phone number or email needed—fully anonymous.
Swiss-based with strong privacy laws.
Best for: Privacy-first group chats.

Element (Matrix Protocol)—element.io

Encrypted, decentralized messaging—does not rely on a single company.
Can be self-hosted for maximum security.
Best for: Secure community spaces and activism groups.

Jitsi Meet—meet.jit.si

Encrypted video conferencing without needing an account.
No data collection, browser-based (no app required).
Best for: Anonymous video meetings.

AVOID: WhatsApp (metadata tracking), Facebook Messenger,
and Telegram (encryption is optional and not default).

A QUEER & TRANS RESOURCE LIST
SECURITY & PRIVACY

SECURE EMAIL SERVICES

ProtonMail—proton.me

End-to-end encrypted email with no logging or tracking.
Swiss-based, strong legal protections.
Best for: Private emails, activism communication.

Tutanota—tutanota.com

Fully encrypted email service based in Germany.
Includes secure calendar & contacts.
Best for: Anonymous email accounts.

AVOID: Gmail, Yahoo, Outlook
(they scan your emails and can be subpoenaed easily).

SECURE WEB BROWSING & ONLINE ANONYMITY

Tor Browser—torproject.org

Routes your internet traffic through multiple servers,
making tracking nearly impossible.
Essential for anonymous research and communication.
Best for: Avoiding surveillance, accessing censored sites.

Brave Browser—brave.com

Blocks trackers, ads, and fingerprinting.
Offers Tor integration for anonymous browsing.
Best for: Private, secure browsing with minimal speed loss.

DuckDuckGo Search—duckduckgo.com

Private search engine that doesn't track searches.
Best for: Searching without Google tracking.

AVOID: Google Chrome (tracks and logs everything),
Microsoft Edge, Safari (less secure).

PASSWORD & EXTRA ACCOUNT SECURITY

Bitwarden—bitwarden.com (Free & Open-Source)

Secure password manager with end-to-end encryption.
Auto-generates strong passwords.
Best for: Keeping all logins secure and unique.

1Password—1password.com *(Paid but excellent security)*

Multi-device password storage with secure sharing features.
Best for: Teams or organizing groups needing shared secure access.

Hardware Security Keys (YubiKey or OnlyKey)—yubico.com / onlykey.io

Most secure way to protect logins (prevents phishing).
Best for: High-risk activists, journalists, and trans organizers.

Mullvad VPN—mullvad.net

Most anonymous VPN (allows cash payments, no account needed).
No logging, no tracking, and based in Sweden (strong privacy laws).
Best for: Avoiding ISP tracking and location masking.

ProtonVPN—protonvpn.com

No logs, Swiss-based, works well with Tor.
Best for: Secure web browsing and accessing censored content.

ANONYMOUS FILE SHARING & STORAGE

OnionShare—onionshare.org

Fully anonymous file-sharing via the Tor network. No central server, no tracking.
Best for: Sharing sensitive documents securely.

CryptPad—cryptpad.fr

Encrypted Google Docs alternative with real-time collaboration.
Best for: Secure activist organizing.